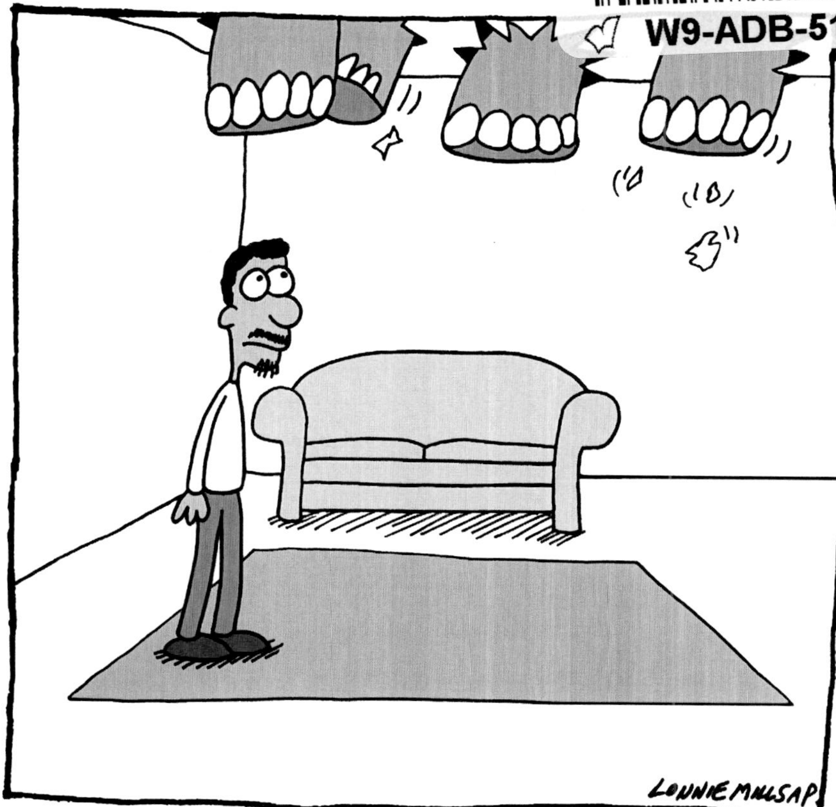
LONNIE MILLSAP

SUDDENLY PETER UNDERSTOOD WHY HIS UPSTAIRS NEIGHBORS WERE ALWAYS SO NOISY

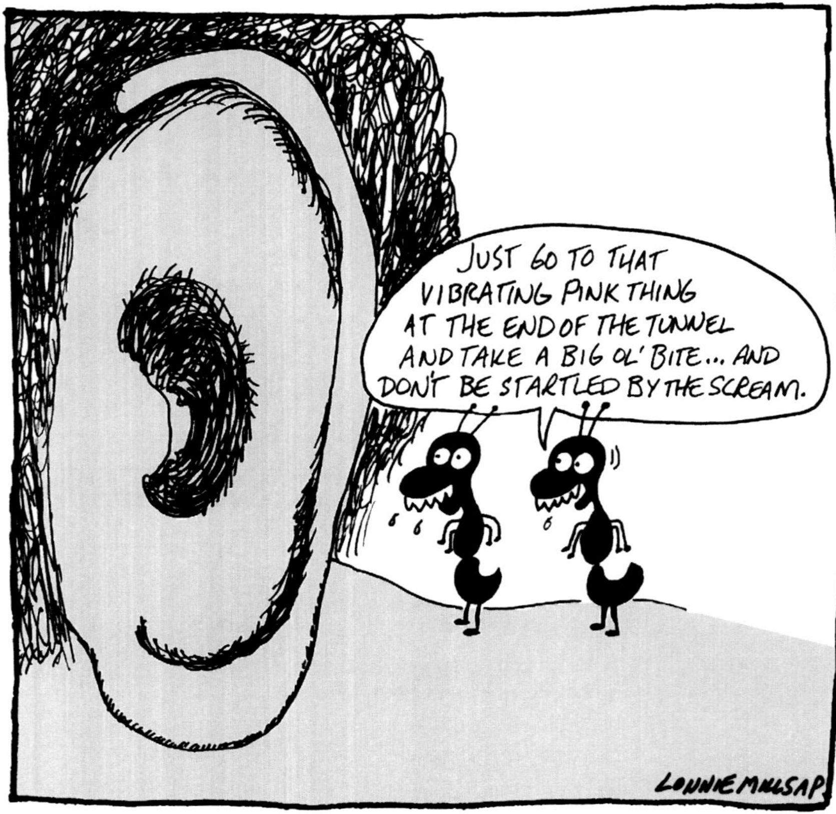
JUST GO TO THAT VIBRATING PINK THING AT THE END OF THE TUNNEL AND TAKE A BIG OL' BITE... AND DON'T BE STARTLED BY THE SCREAM.
LONNIE MILLSAP

MY WASHCLOTH STINKS!

BY
LONNIE MILLSAP

ROLLYHEAD PUBLISHING

SPECIAL THANKS TO MY MOTHER, MY FATHER, MY FRIENDS, MY RELATIVES AND EVERYONE WHO LAUGHED (OR GROANED) AT MY CARTOONS EVERY ONCE IN A WHILE...OR NOT. OH, AND A VERY SPECIAL THANKS TO YOLANDA. COMPLETING THIS BOOK LEAVES MY LIFE WITH ONE LESS "WHAT IF?"

...AND TO EVERYONE WHOSE WASHCLOTH STINKS, USE A LITTLE AMMONIA DURING THE WASH CYCLE.

Rollyhead Publishing, Inc., 215 North Avenue #3508, Atlanta, Georgia, 30308. All contents ©2009 Lonnie J. Millsap III. All rights reserved. No part of this book may be reprinted without written permission from the author or publisher, except for review purposes as defined by the laws of jounalistic Fair Use. No similarity between any of the names, characters, persons and institutions in My Washcloth Stinks! and those of any living or dead persons is intended and any such similarity that may exist is purely coincidental. Published by Rollyhead Publishing, Inc. Edited & Promoted by Lonnie Millsap. Art Direction & Color by Lonnie J. Millsap. Cover design by Lonnie Millsap. Production by Lonnie Millsap. First Printing: November 2009. ISBN: 978-0-9843289-0-1. Printed in USA by Graphic Visions Unlimited, 800 Port 14 Place, Atlanta, GA.

Visit www.lonniemillsap.com for more work by the author!

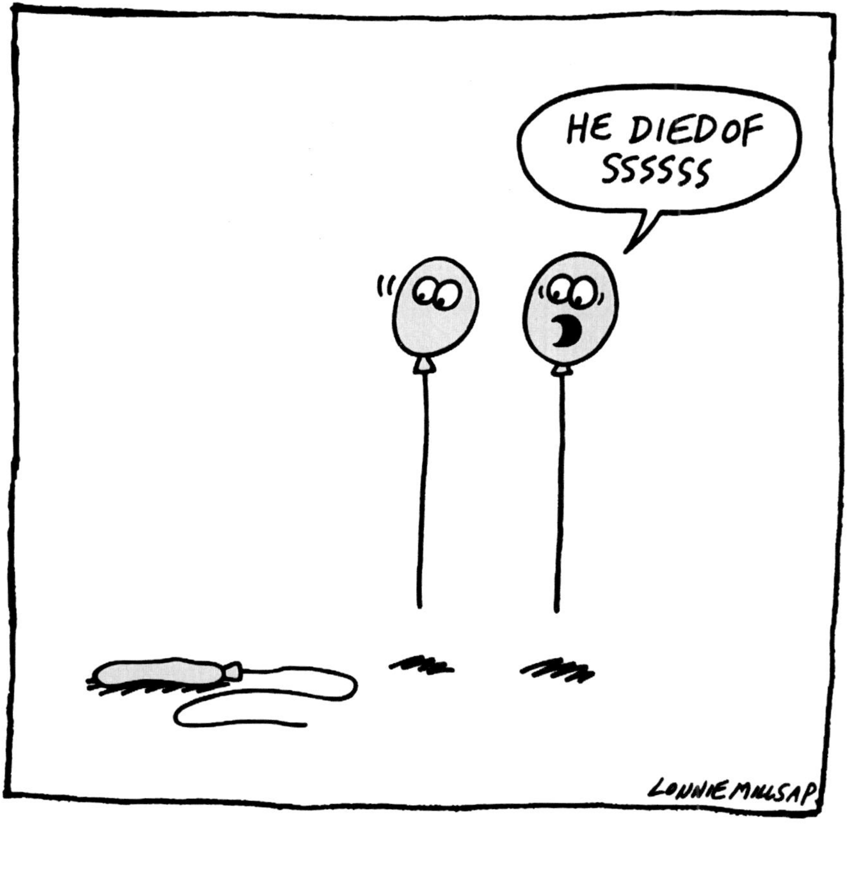
HE DIED OF SSSSSS
LONNIE MILLSAP

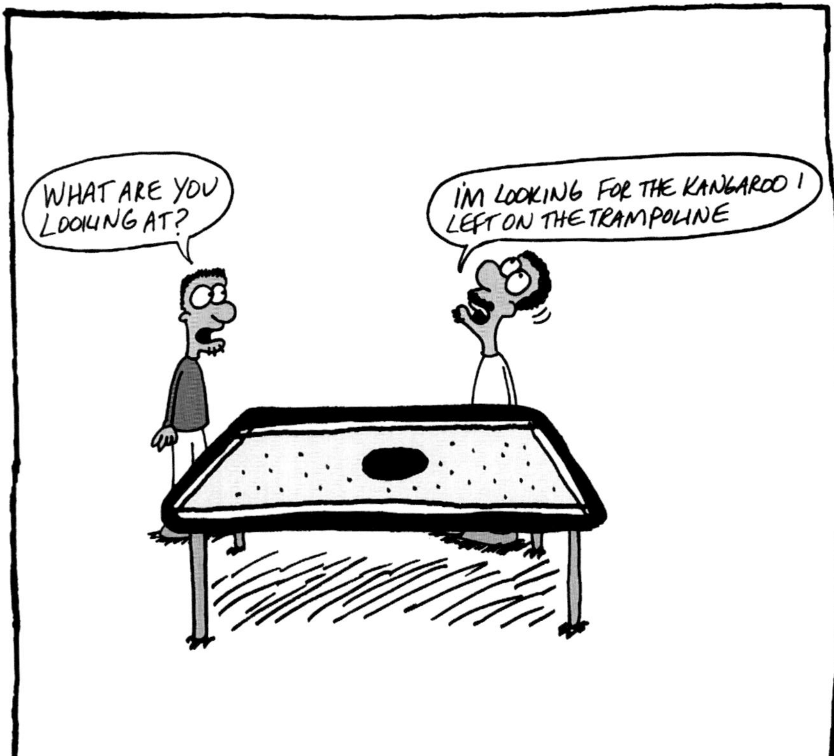
WHAT ARE YOU LOOKING AT?
I'M LOOKING FOR THE KANGAROO I LEFT ON THE TRAMPOLINE
LONNIE MILLSAP

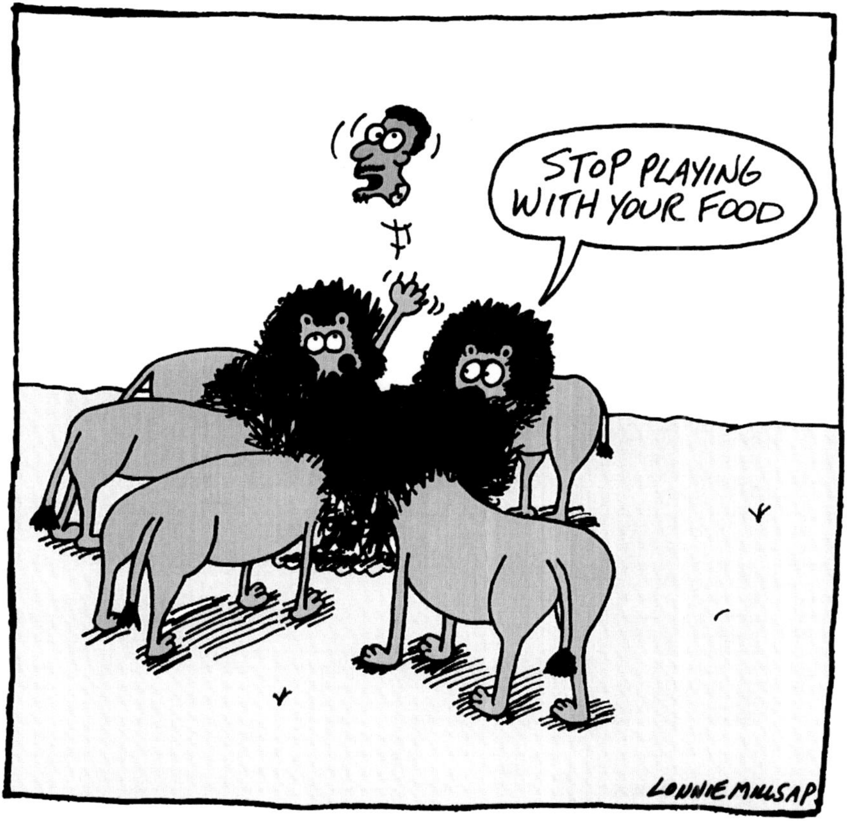
STOP PLAYING WITH YOUR FOOD
LONNIE MILLSAP

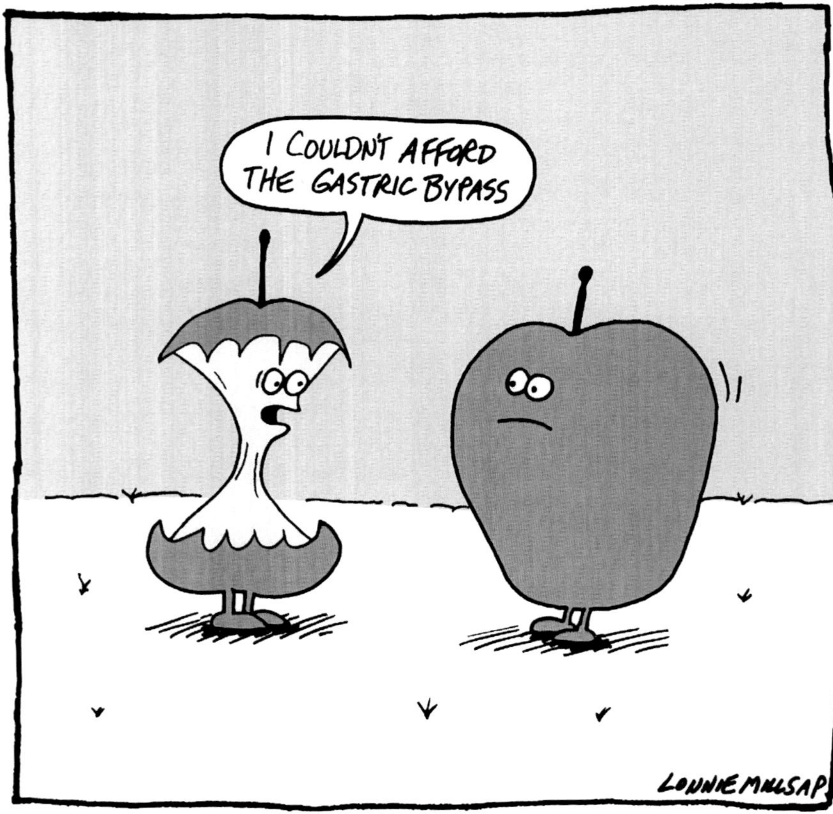
I COULDN'T AFFORD THE GASTRIC BYPASS
LONNIE MILLSAP

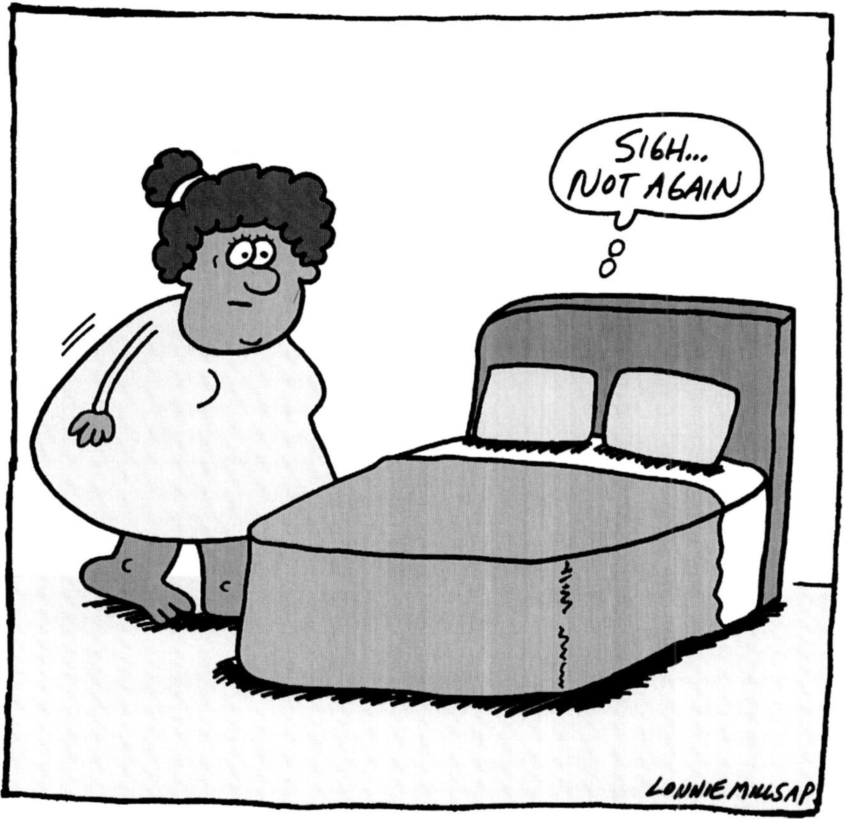
SIGH...
NOT AGAIN
LONNIE MILLSAP

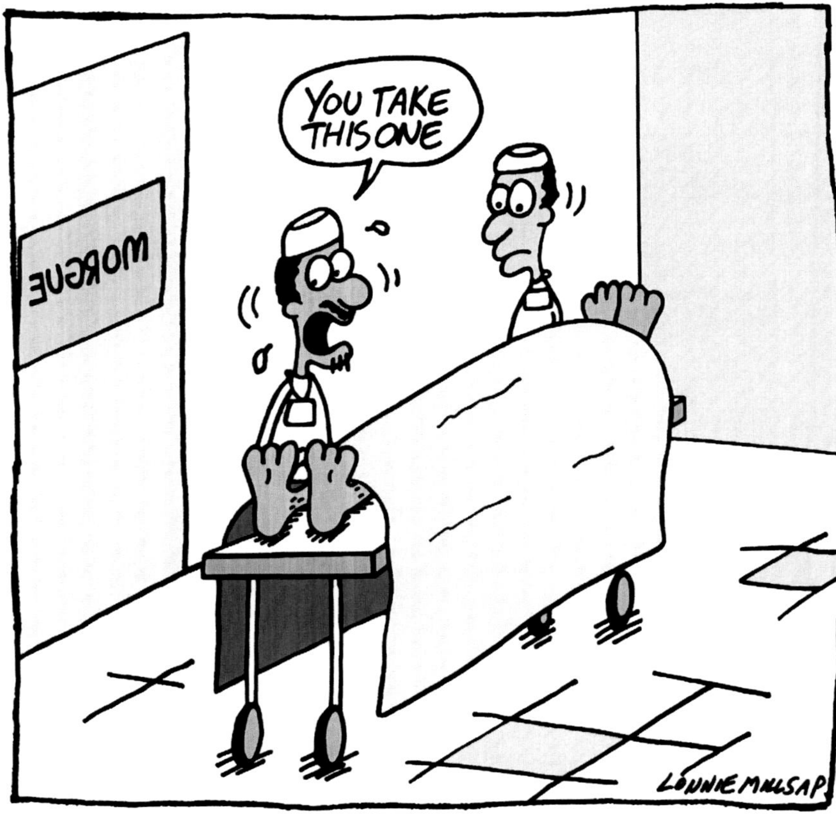
MORGUE
YOU TAKE THIS ONE
LONNIE MILLSAP

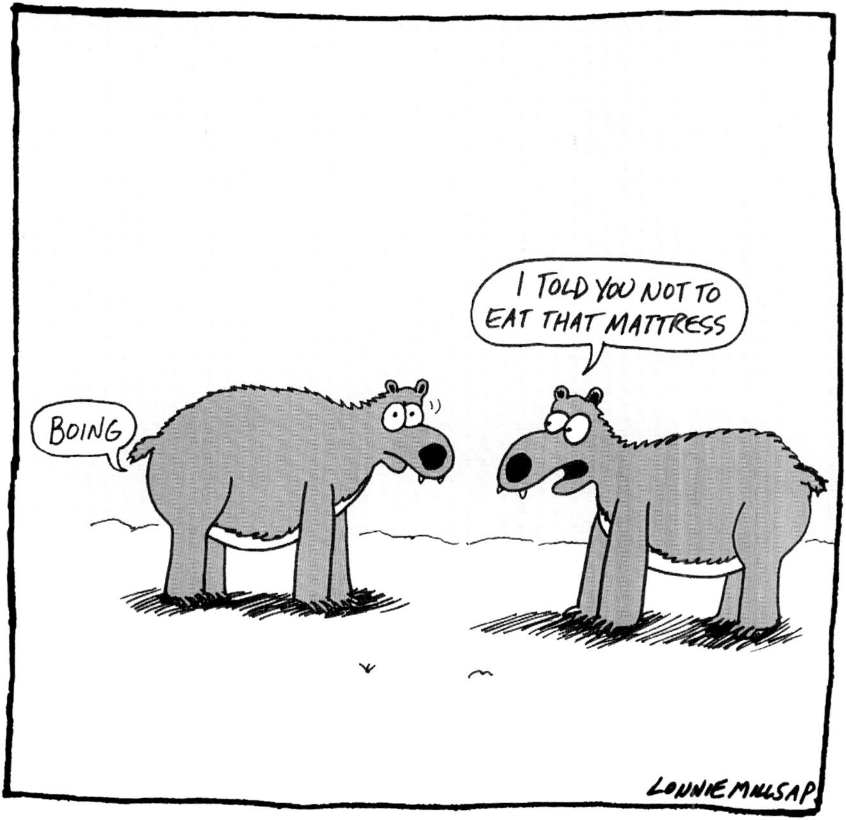
BOING
I TOLD YOU NOT TO EAT THAT MATTRESS
LONNIE MILLSAP

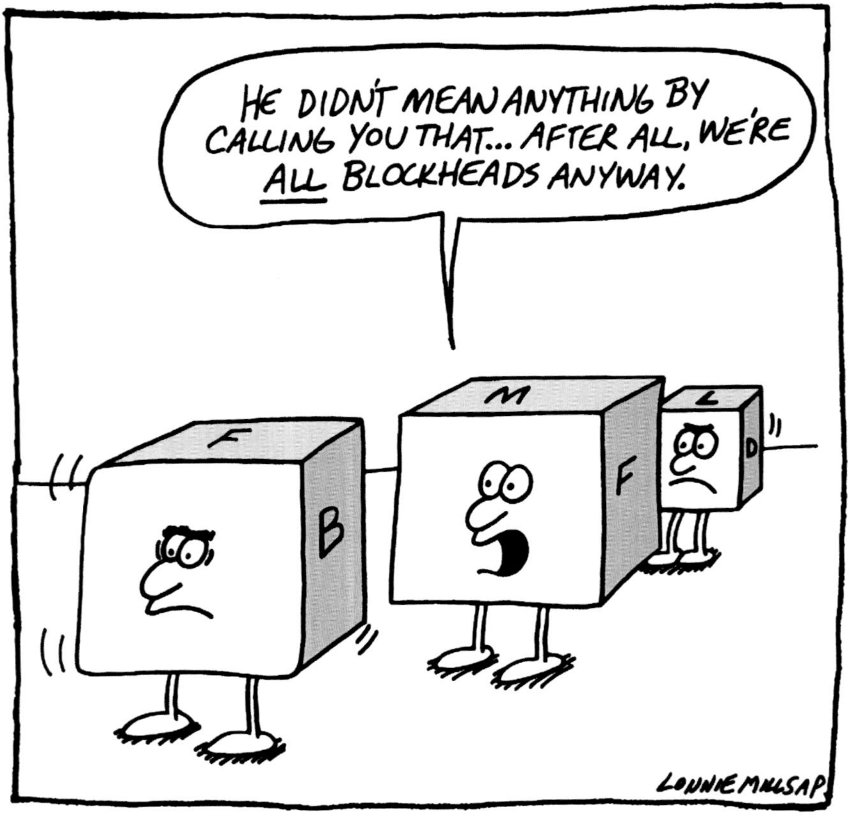
HE DIDN'T MEAN ANYTHING BY CALLING YOU THAT... AFTER ALL, WE'RE ALL BLOCKHEADS ANYWAY.
F
B
M
F
L
D
LONNIE MILLSAP

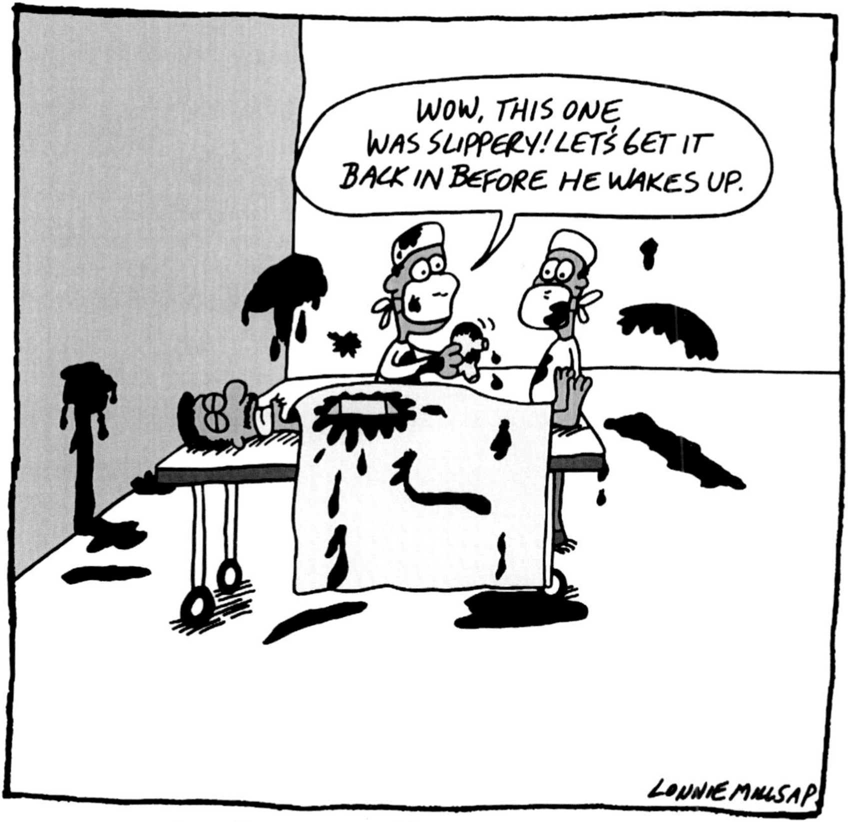
WOW, THIS ONE WAS SLIPPERY! LET'S GET IT BACK IN BEFORE HE WAKES UP.
LONNIE MILLSAP

WHAT REALLY HAPPENS DURING SURGERY

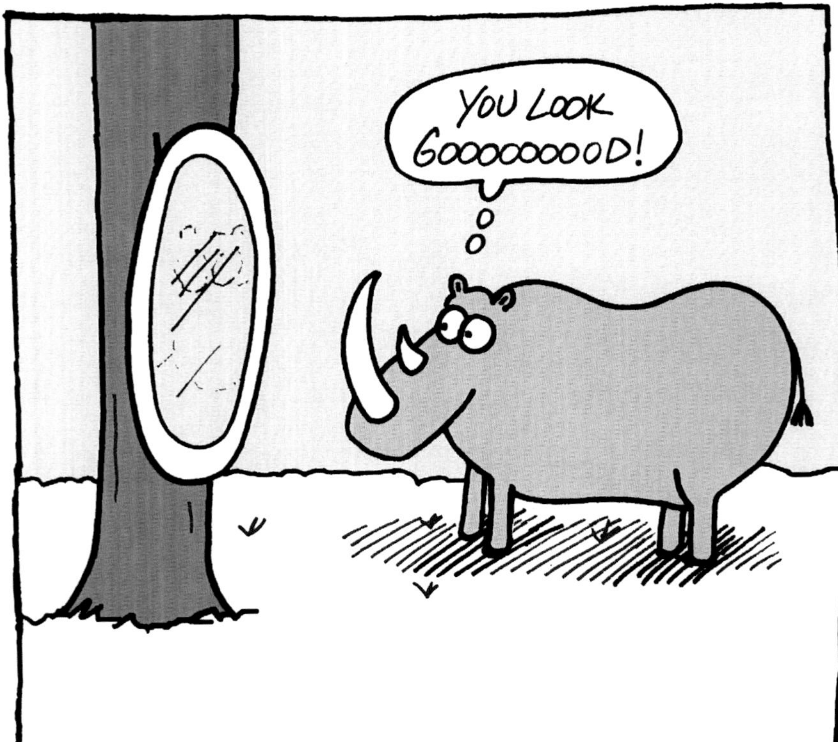
YOU LOOK GOOOOOOOOOD!
LONNIE MILLSAP

RHINARCISSIST

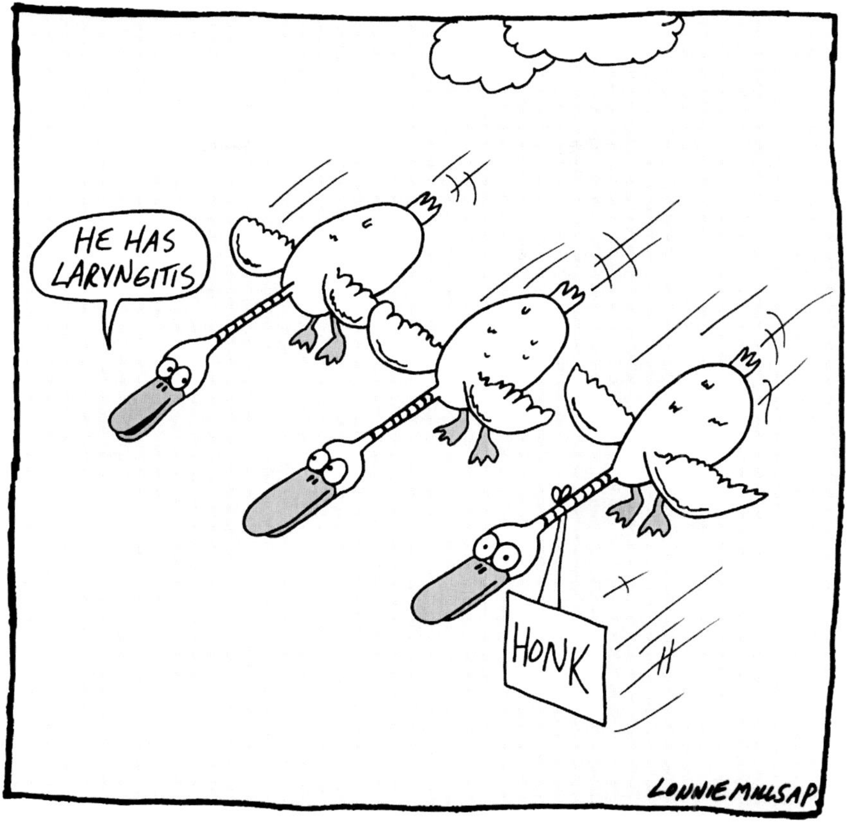
HE HAS LARYNGITIS
HONK
LONNIE MILLSAP

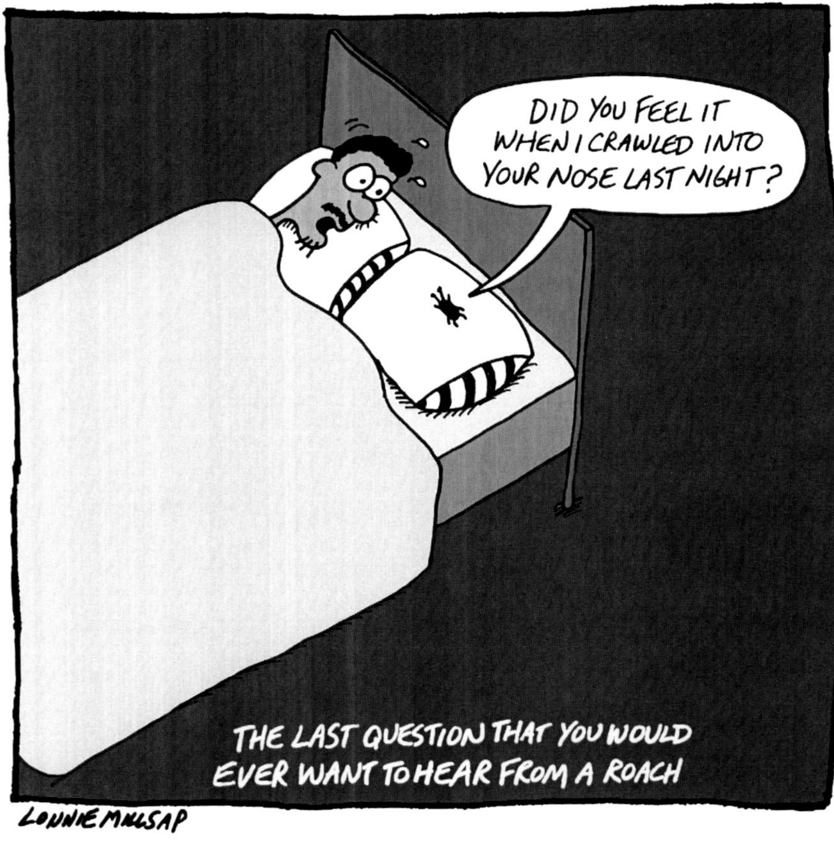
DID YOU FEEL IT WHEN I CRAWLED INTO YOUR NOSE LAST NIGHT?
THE LAST QUESTION THAT YOU WOULD EVER WANT TO HEAR FROM A ROACH
LONNIE MILLSAP

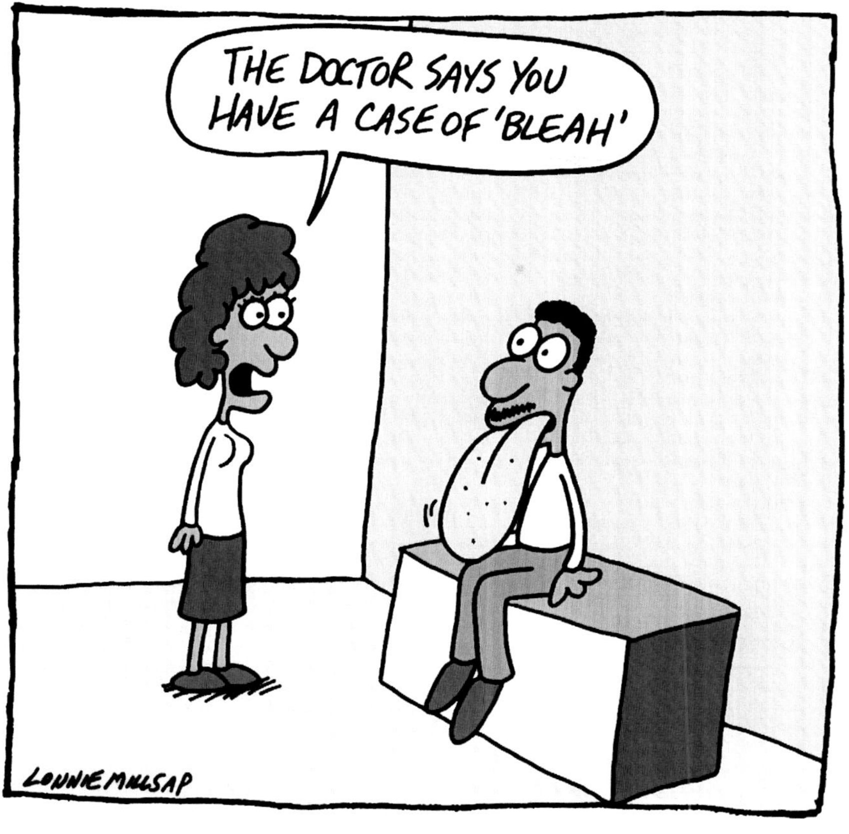
THE DOCTOR SAYS YOU HAVE A CASE OF 'BLEAH'
LONNIE MILLSAP

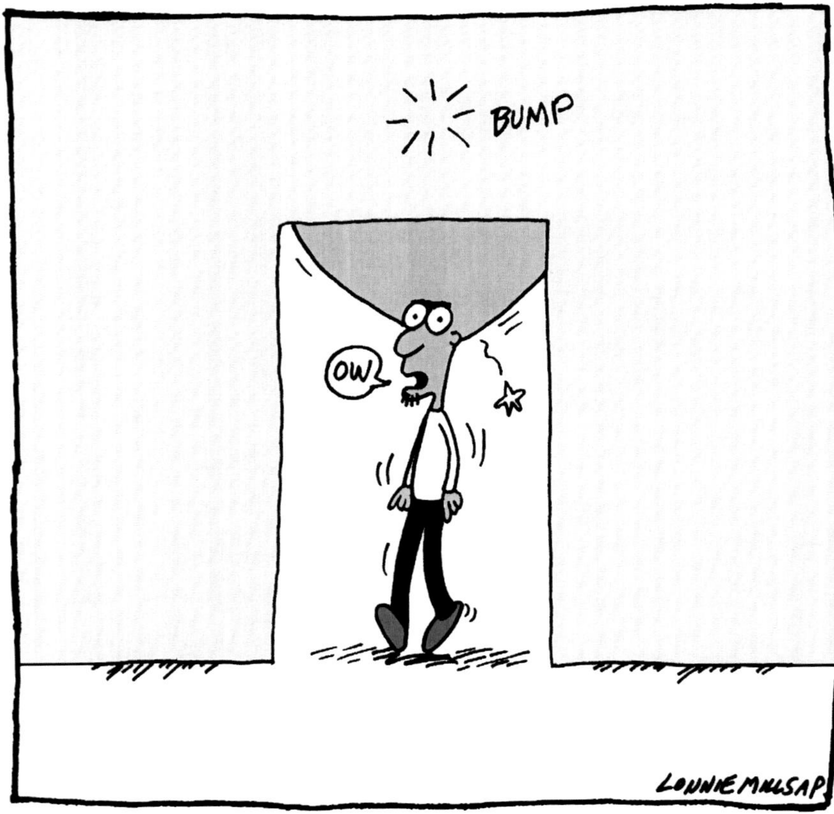
BUMP
OW
LONNIE MILLSAP

JUST ANOTHER DAY ON
PLANET MEGACEPHALIC

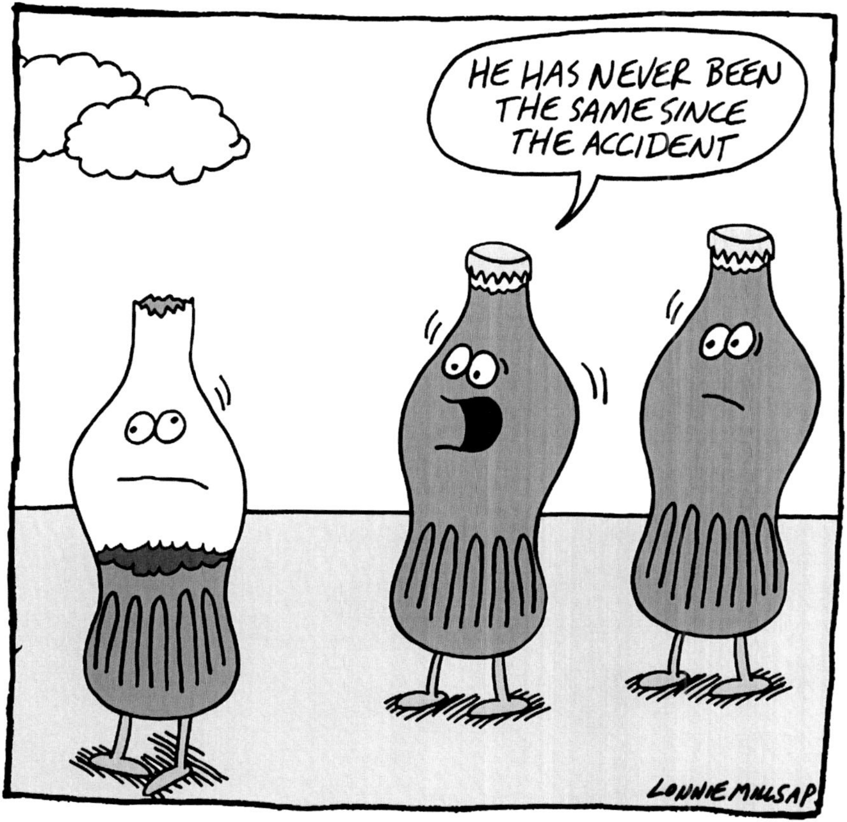
HE HAS NEVER BEEN THE SAME SINCE THE ACCIDENT
LONNIE MILLSAP

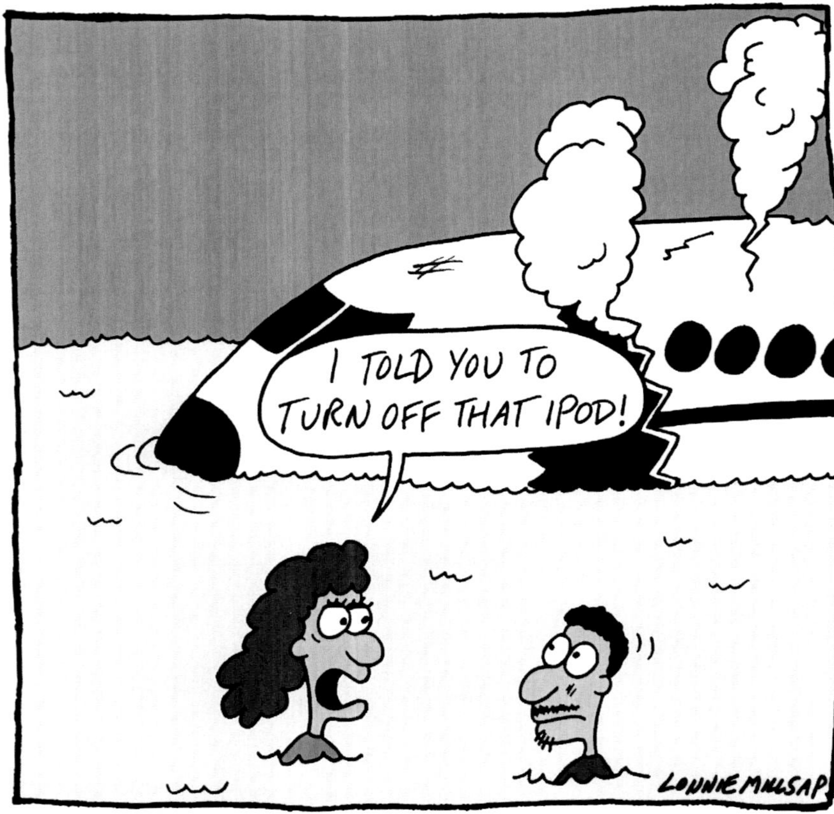
I TOLD YOU TO TURN OFF THAT IPOD!
LONNIE MILLSAP

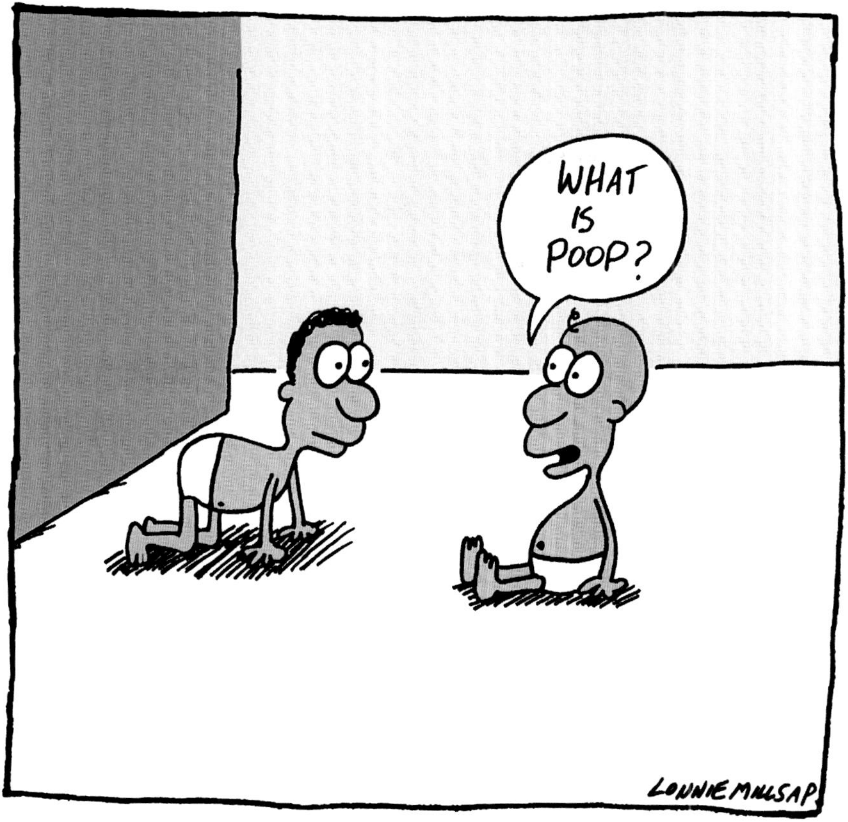
WHAT IS POOP?
LONNIE MILLSAP

INFANT JEOPARDY

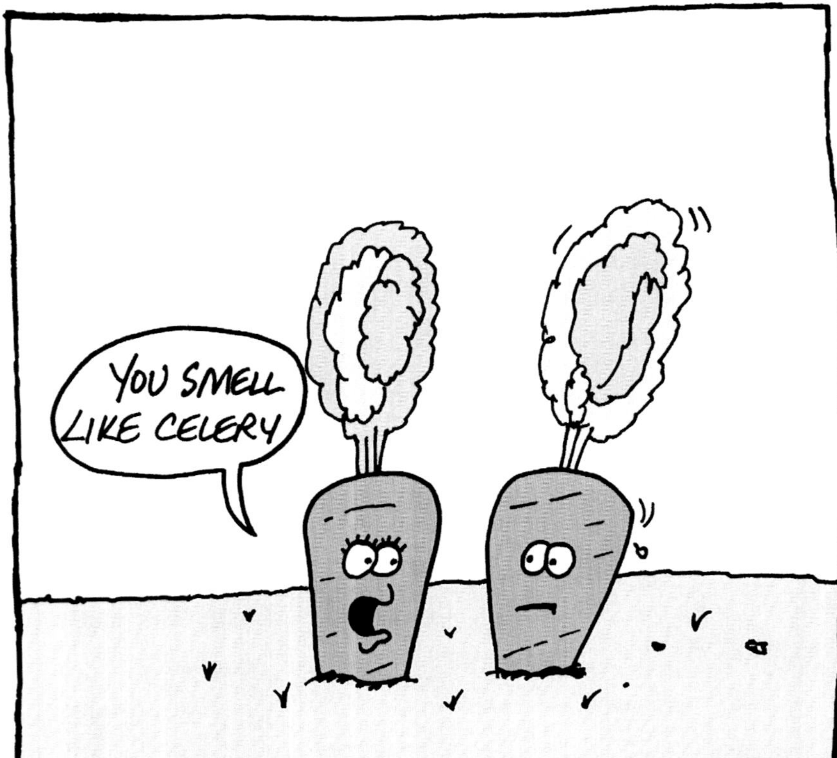
YOU SMELL LIKE CELERY
LONNIE MILLSAP

WHEN CARROTS CHEAT

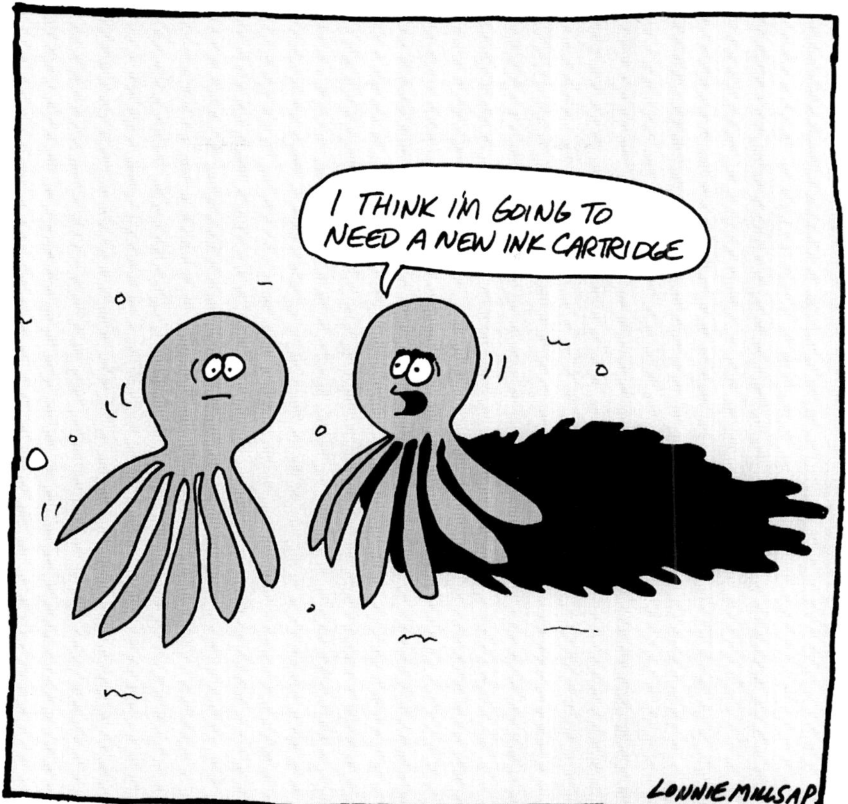
I THINK I'M GOING TO NEED A NEW INK CARTRIDGE
LONNIE MILLSAP

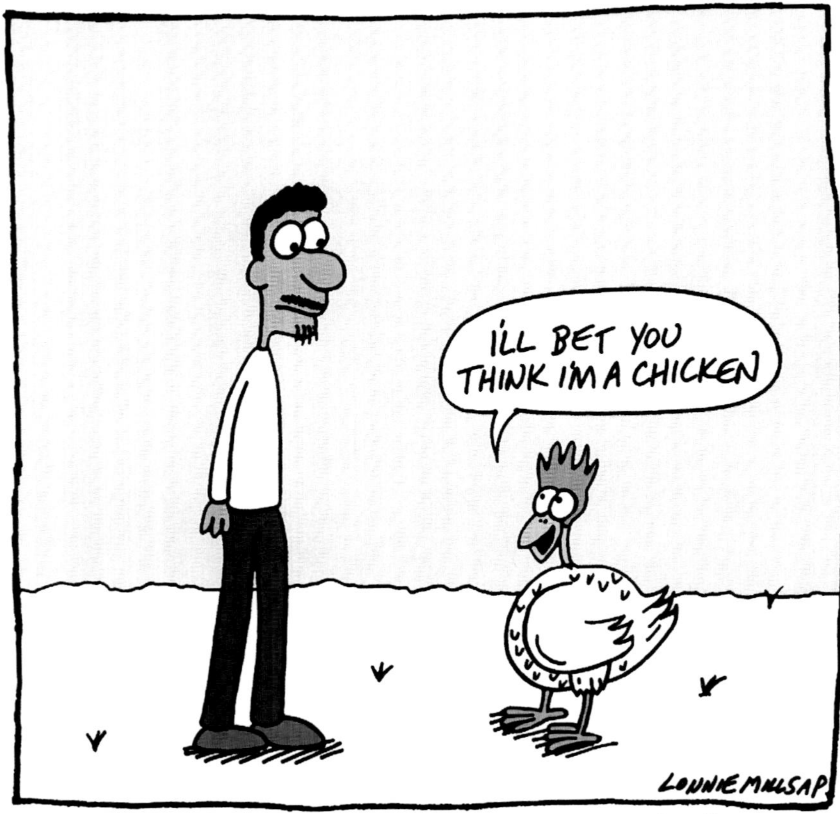
I'LL BET YOU THINK I'M A CHICKEN
LONNIE MILLSAP
BOB FOUND OUT 20 MINUTES LATER THAT IT DAMN SURE TASTED LIKE CHICKEN

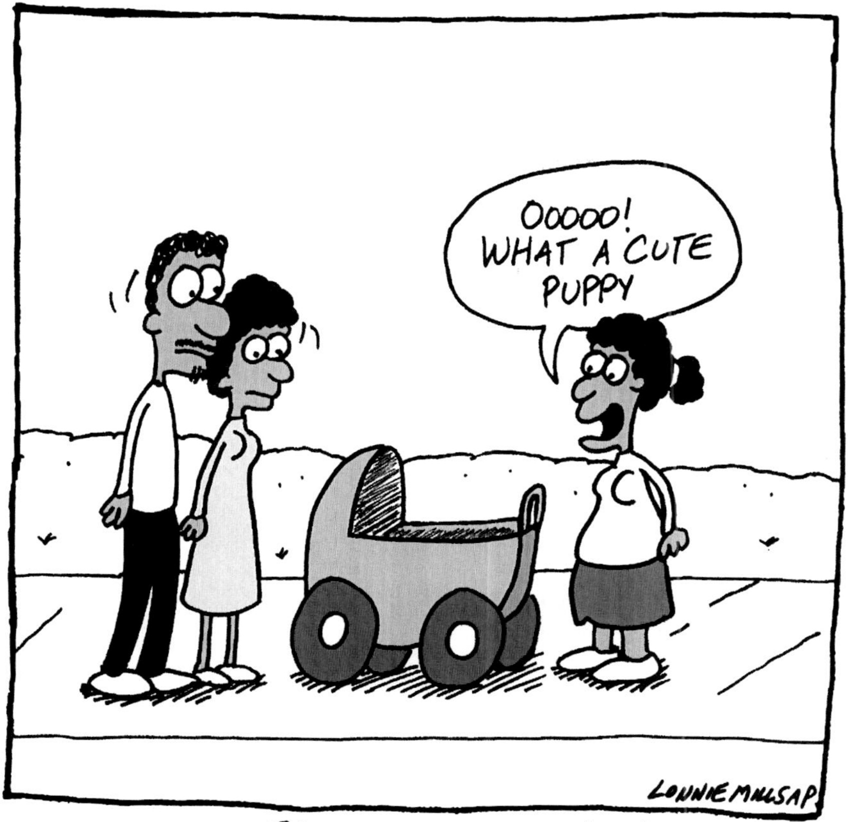
OOOOO! WHAT A CUTE PUPPY
LONNIE MILLSAP

THE LAST THING NEW PARENTS WANT TO HEAR

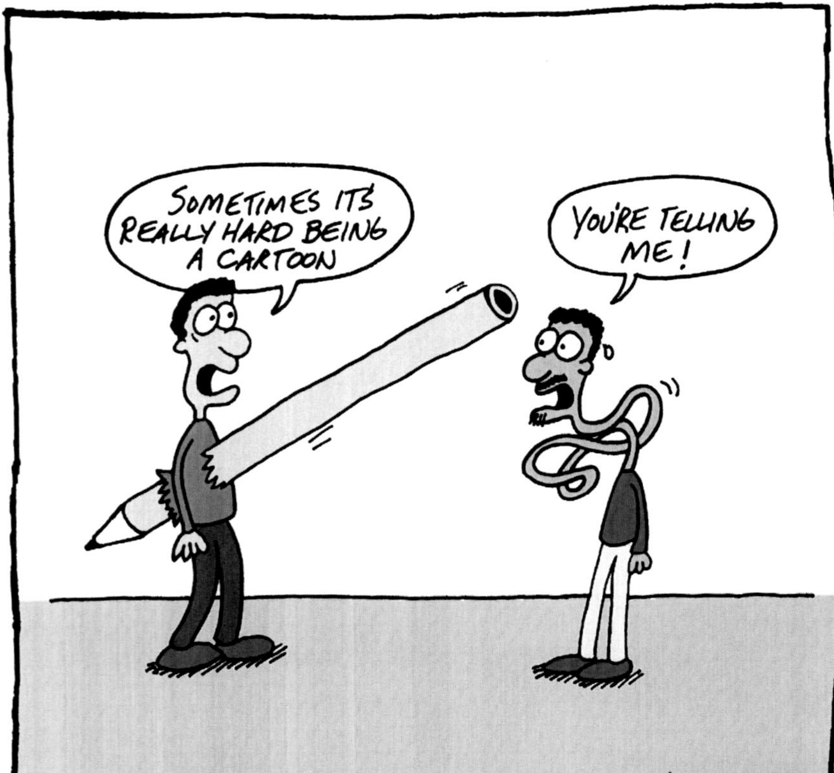
SOMETIMES IT'S REALLY HARD BEING A CARTOON
YOU'RE TELLING ME!
LONNIE MILLSAP

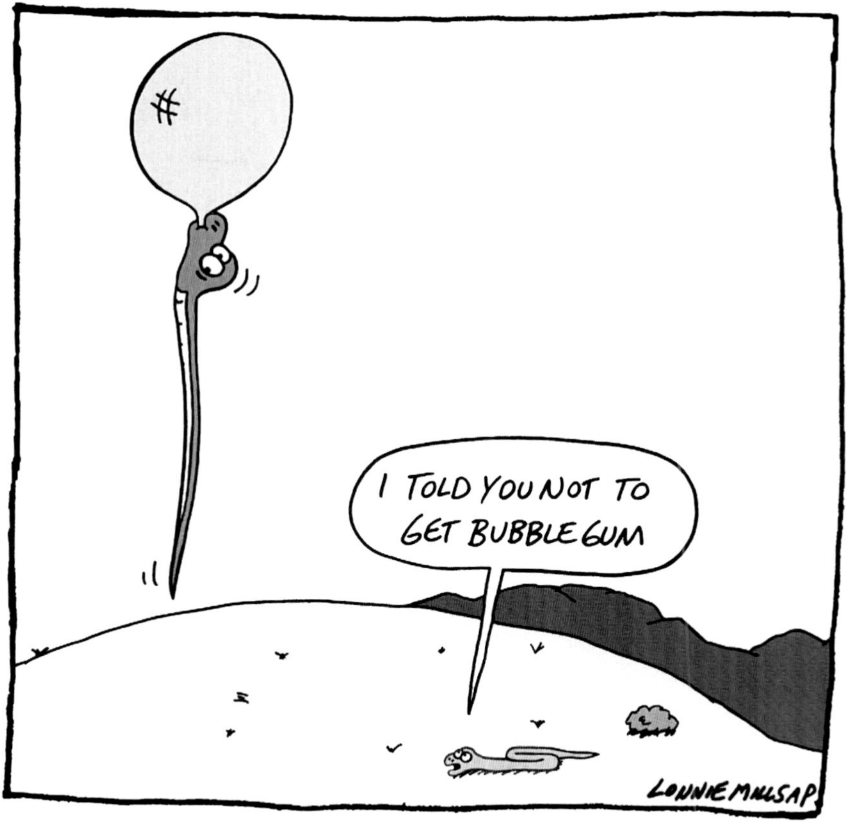
I TOLD YOU NOT TO GET BUBBLE GUM
LONNIE MILLSAP

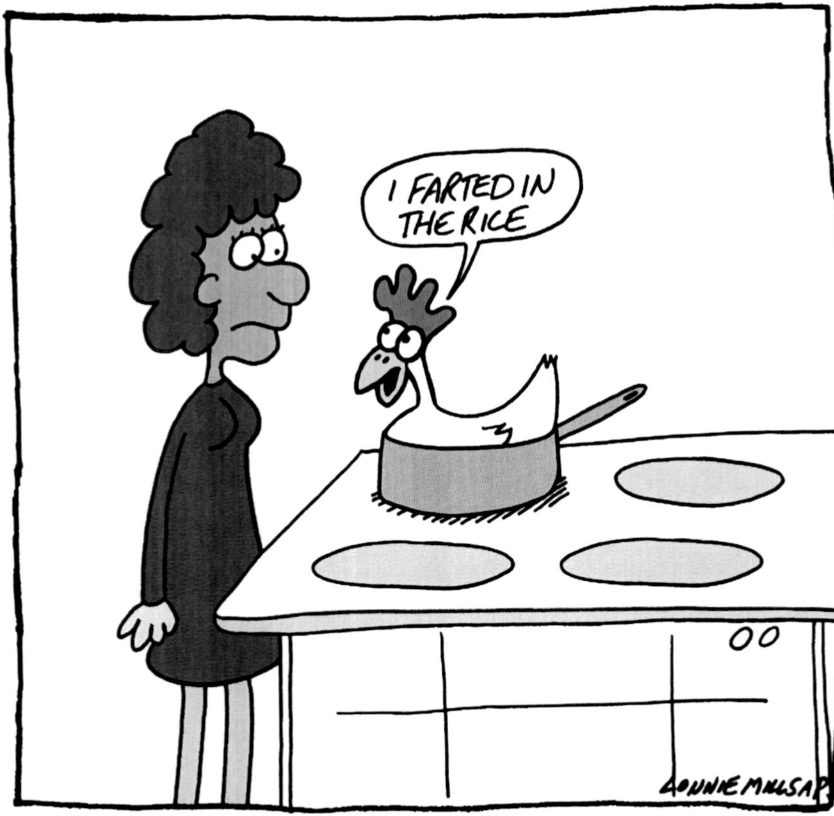
I FARTED IN THE RICE
LONNIE MILLSAP
CHICKEN AND RICE COOKING TIP: KILL THE CHICKEN BEFORE YOU ADD IT TO THE RICE

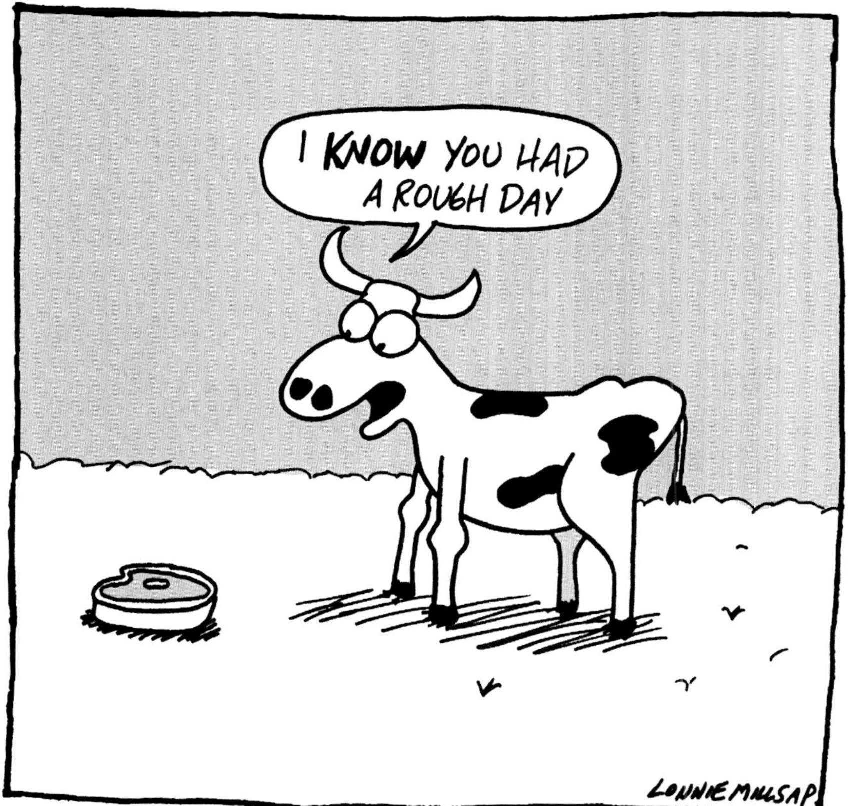
I KNOW YOU HAD A ROUGH DAY
LONNIE MILLSAP

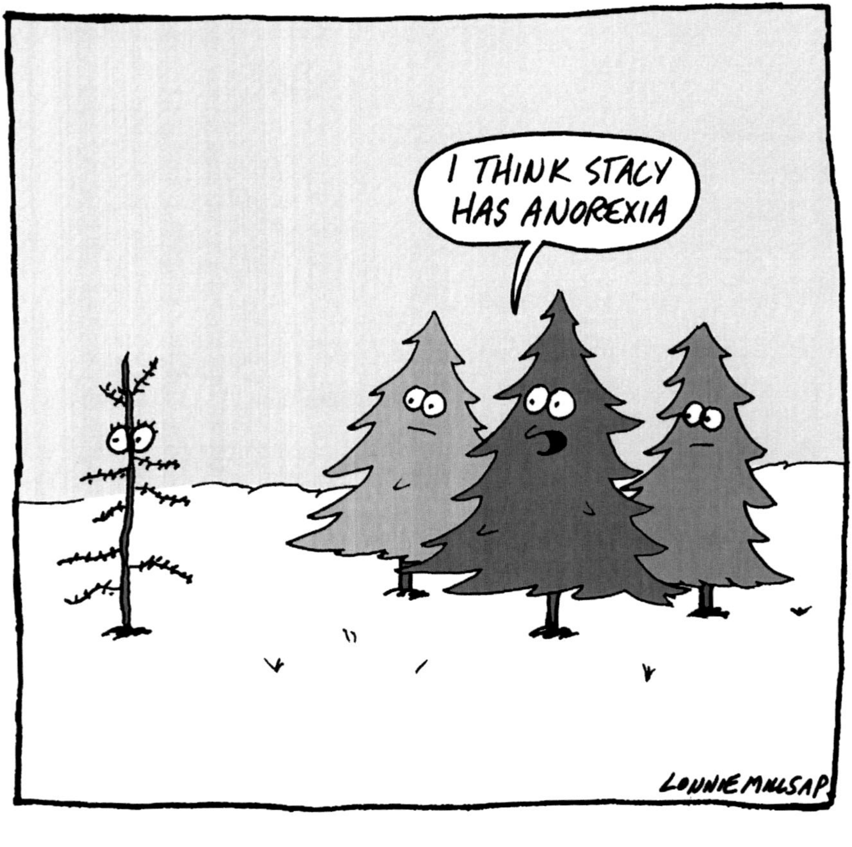
I THINK STACY HAS ANOREXIA
LONNIE MILLSAP

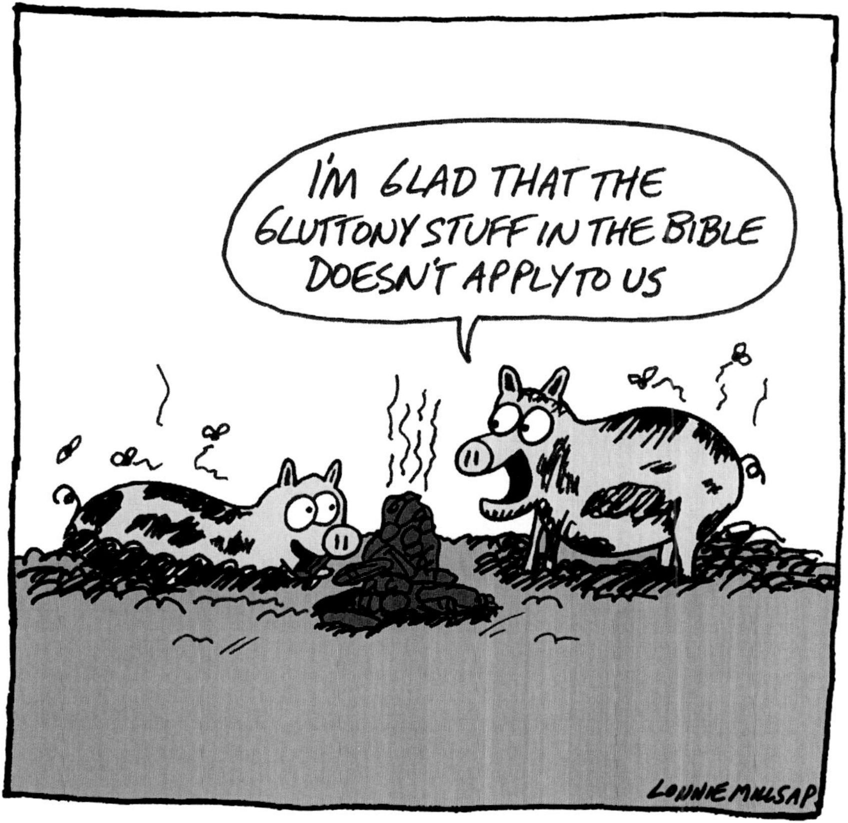
I'M GLAD THAT THE GLUTTONY STUFF IN THE BIBLE DOESN'T APPLY TO US
LONNIE MILLSAP

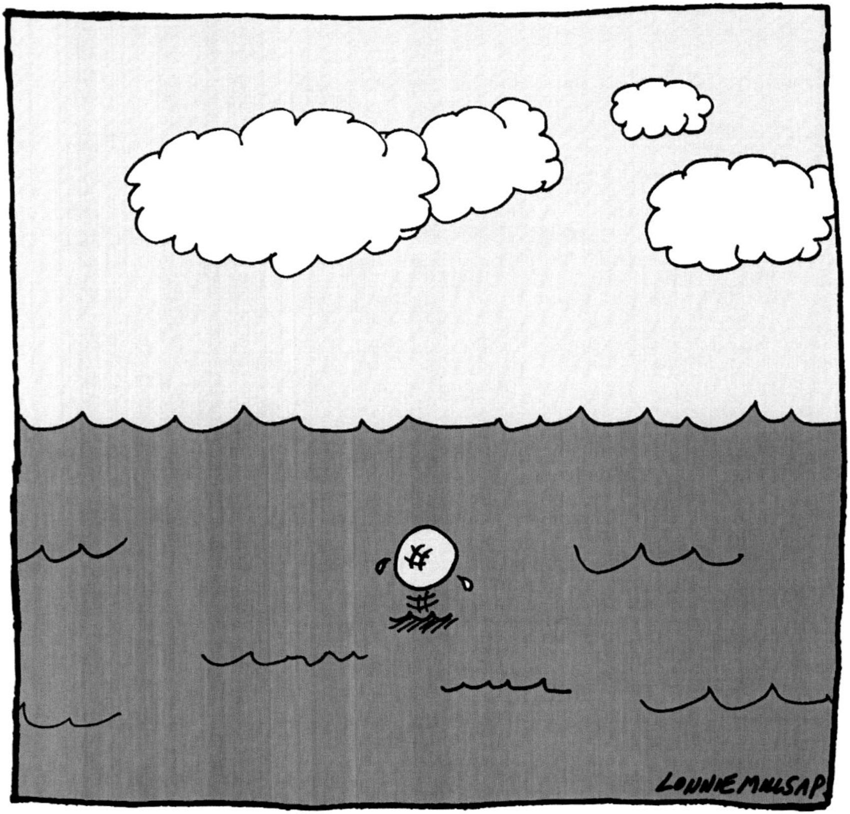
LONNIE MILLSAP

WHEN FISH FART

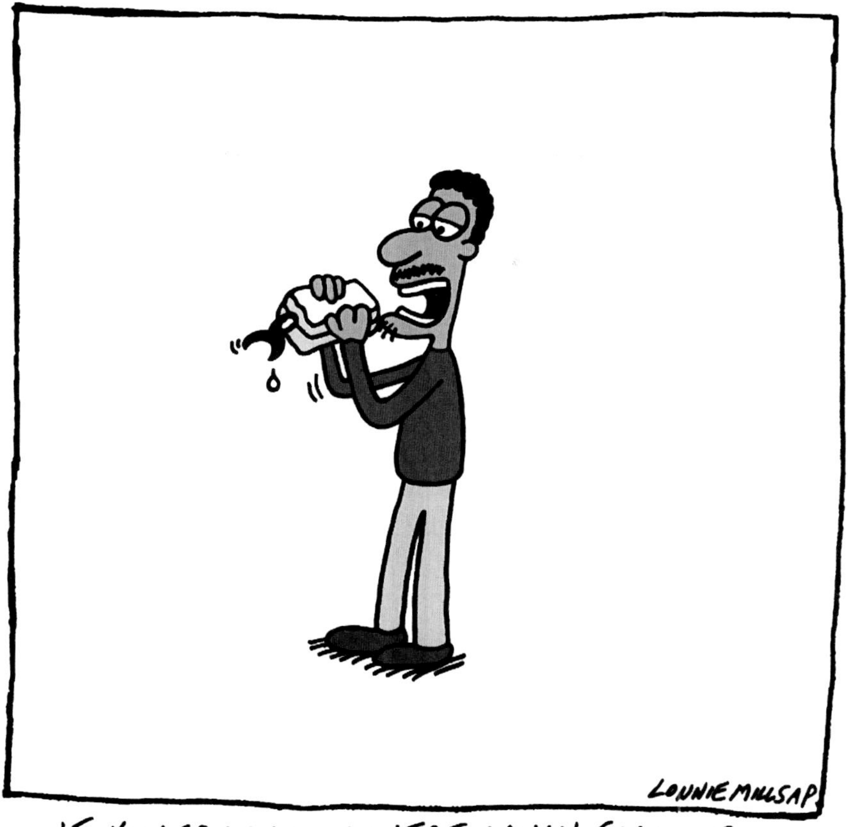
LONNIE MILLSAP

IF KILLER WHALES WERE MUCH SMALLER

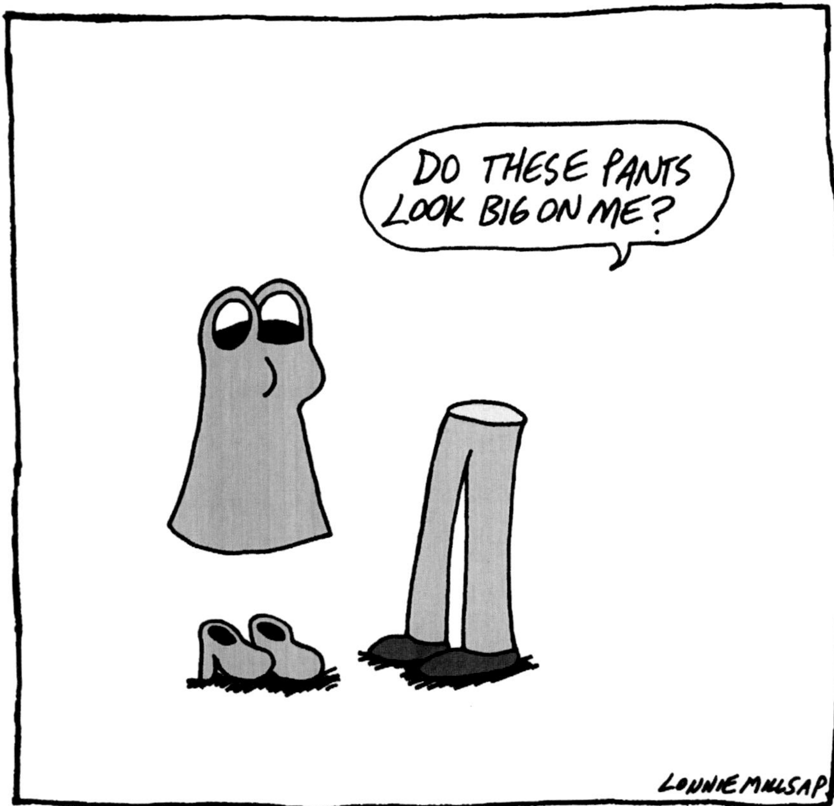
DO THESE PANTS LOOK BIG ON ME?
LONNIE MILLSAP

ANOTHER USELESS QUESTION FROM THE INVSIBLE MAN

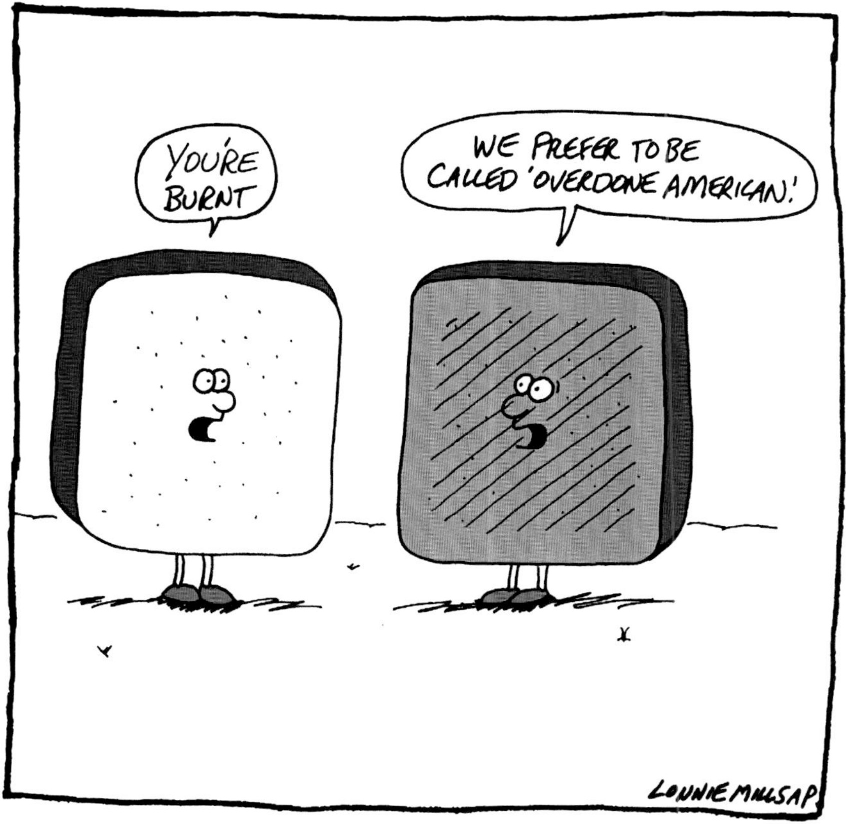
YOU'RE BURNT
WE PREFER TO BE CALLED 'OVERDONE AMERICAN.'
LONNIE MILLSAP

POLITICAL CORRECTNESS IN THE TOAST COMMUNITY

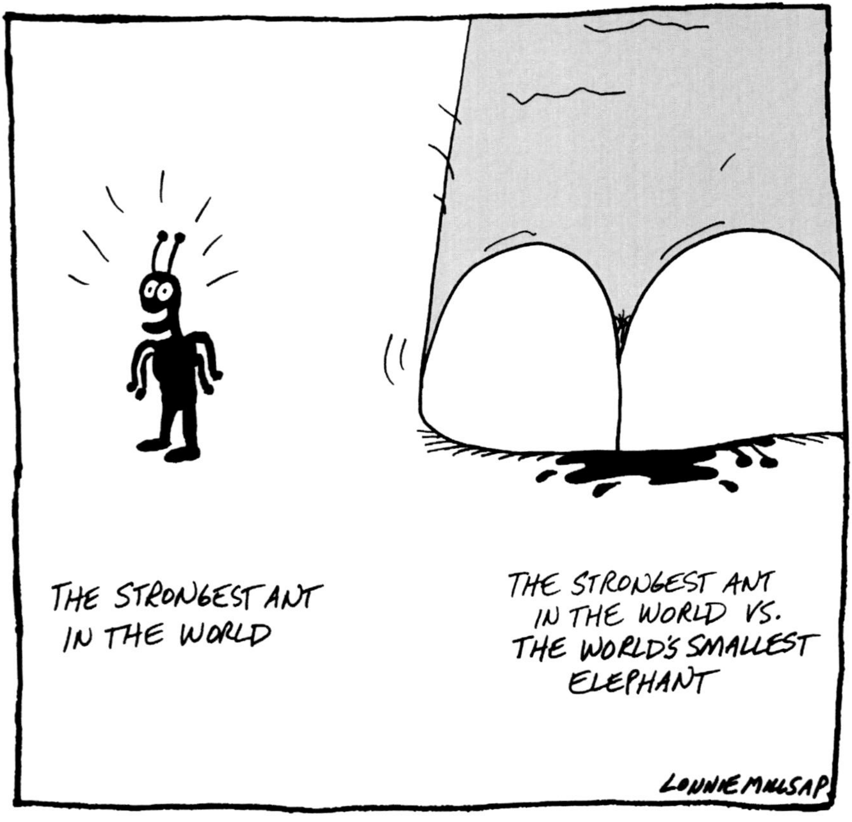
THE STRONGEST ANT IN THE WORLD
THE STRONGEST ANT IN THE WORLD VS. THE WORLD'S SMALLEST ELEPHANT
LONNIE MILLSAP

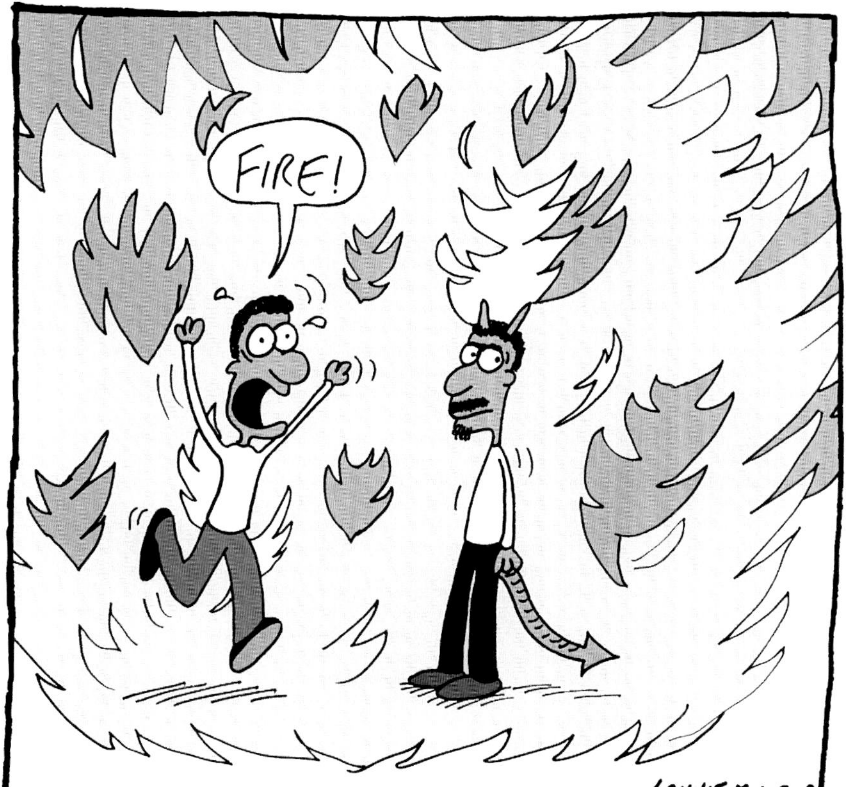
FIRE!
LONNIE MILLSAP

MEANINGLESS ALERTS IN HELL

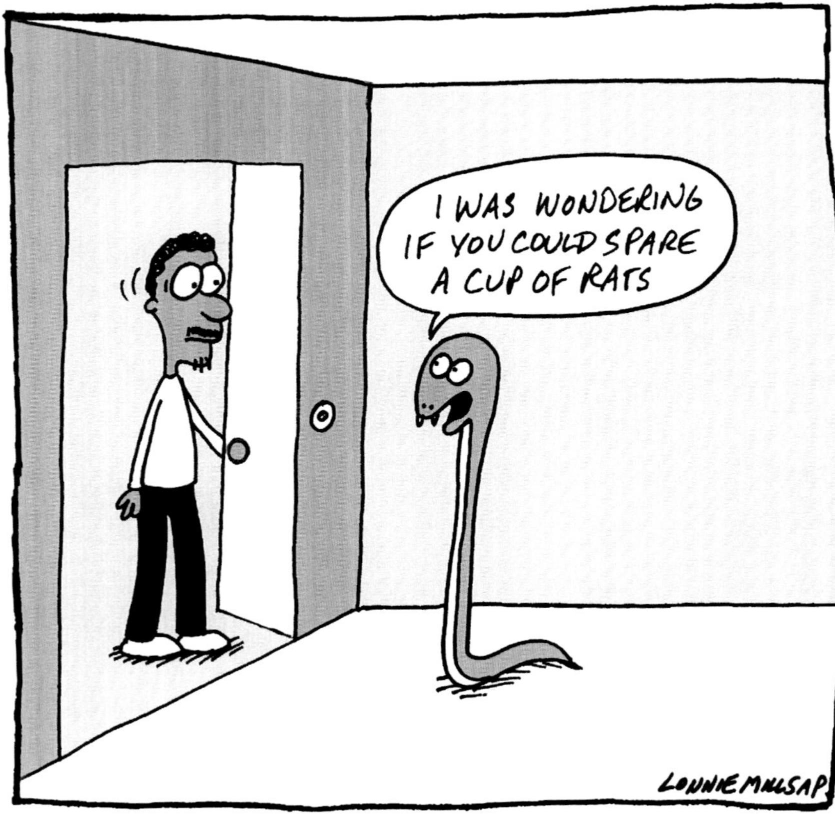
I WAS WONDERING IF YOU COULD SPARE A CUP OF RATS
LONNIE MILLSAP

CROSS SPECIES APARTMENT LIVING

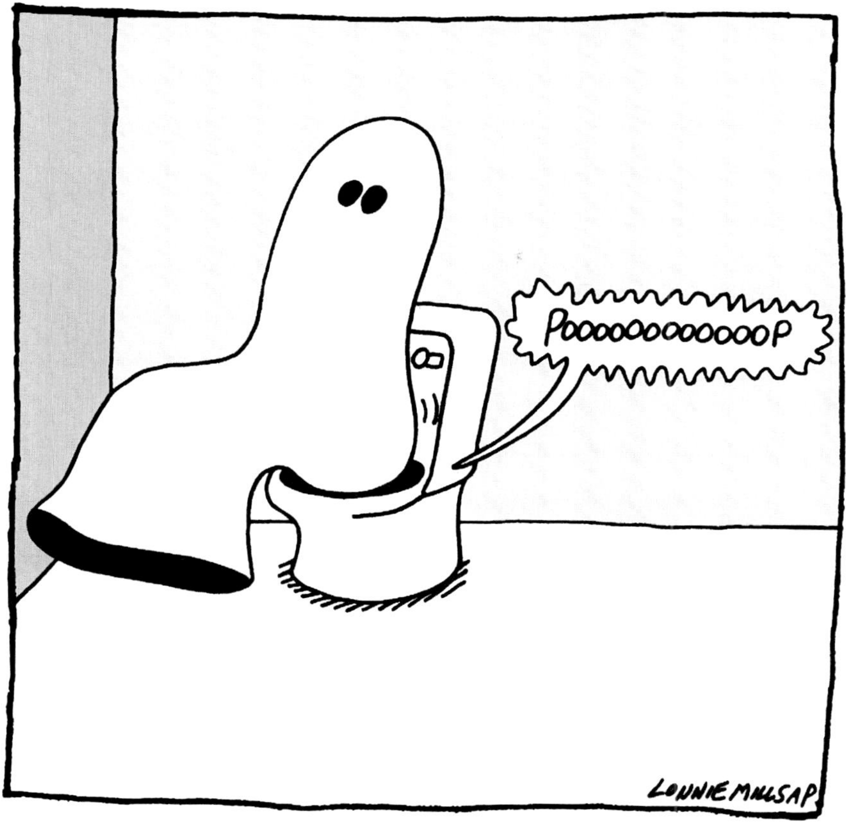
POOOOOOOOOOOOOP
LONNIE MILLSAP

WHEN GHOSTS GOTTA GO

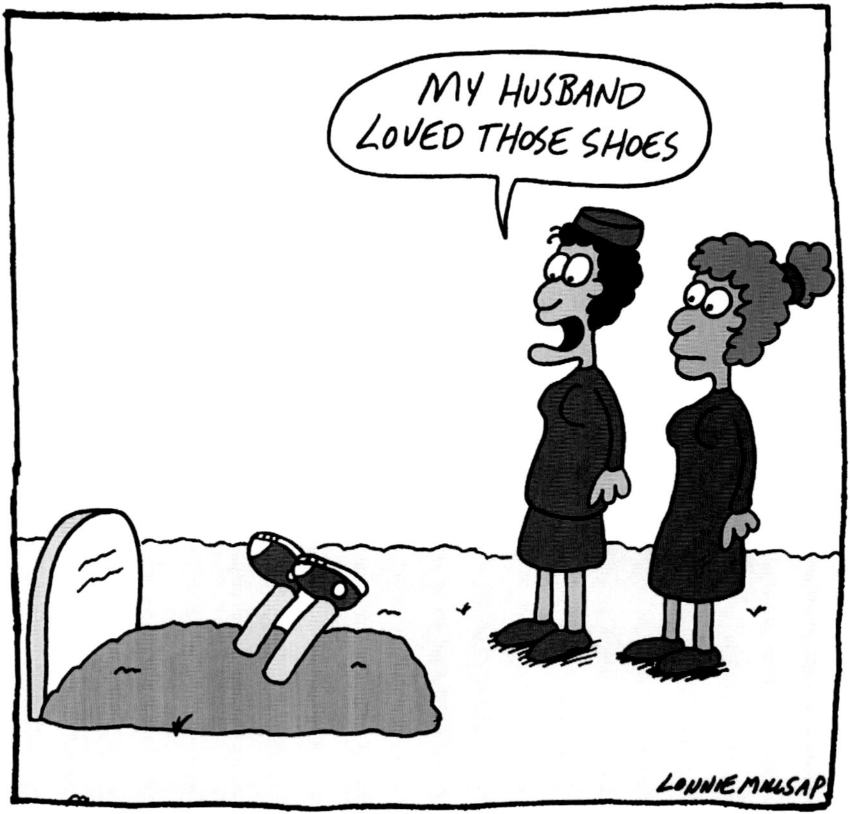
MY HUSBAND LOVED THOSE SHOES
LONNIE MILLSAP

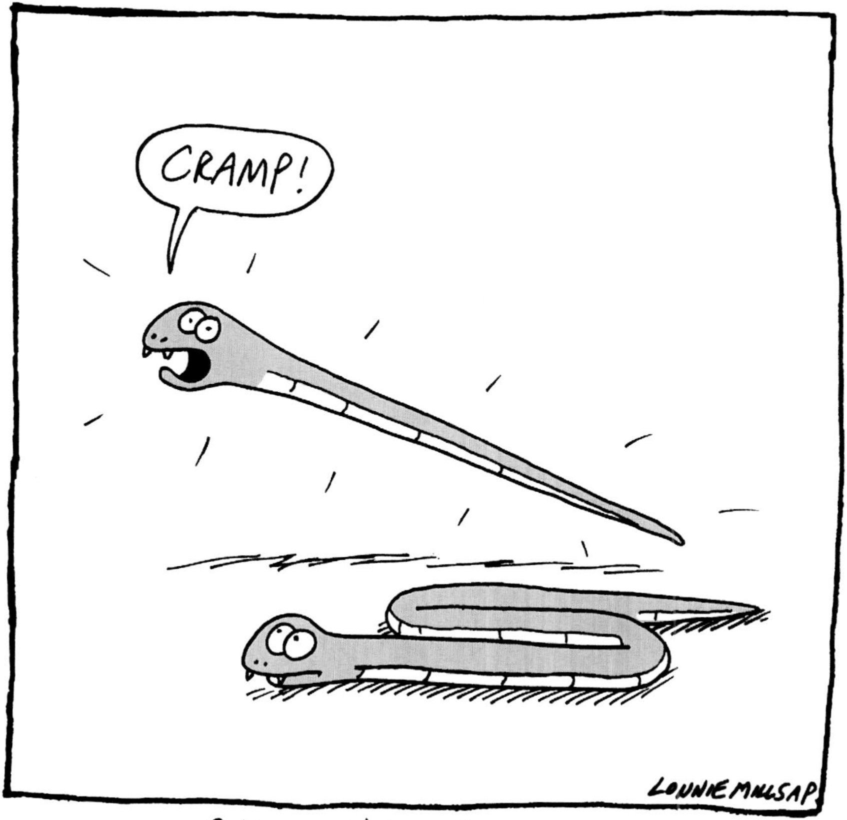
CRAMP!
LONNIE MILLSAP

SNAKES NEED POTASSIUM TOO

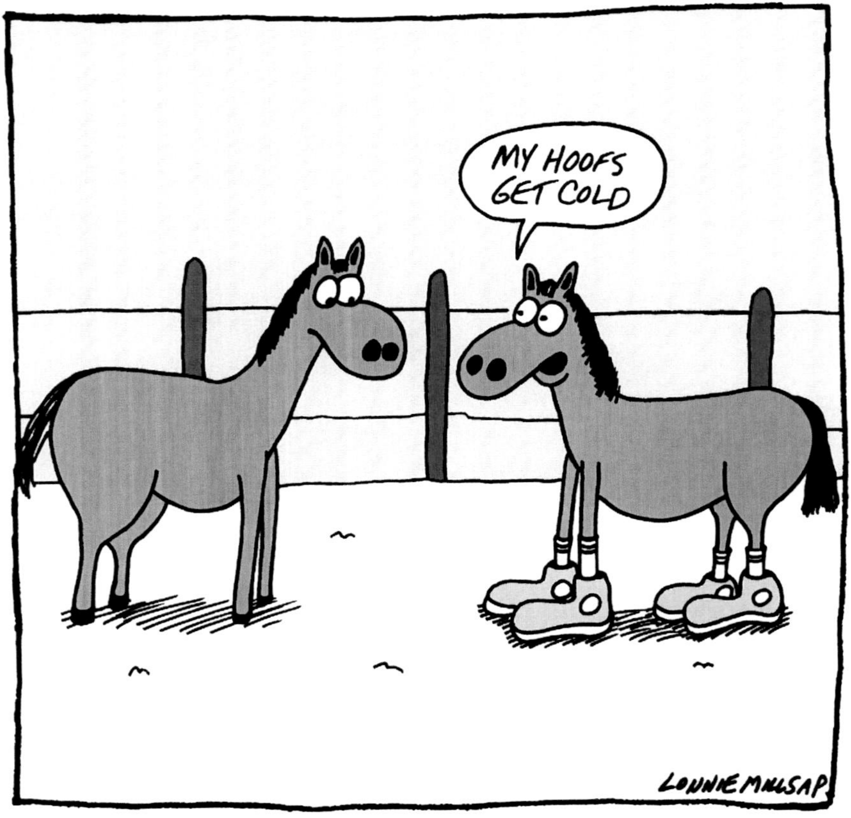
MY HOOFS GET COLD
LONNIE MILLSAP

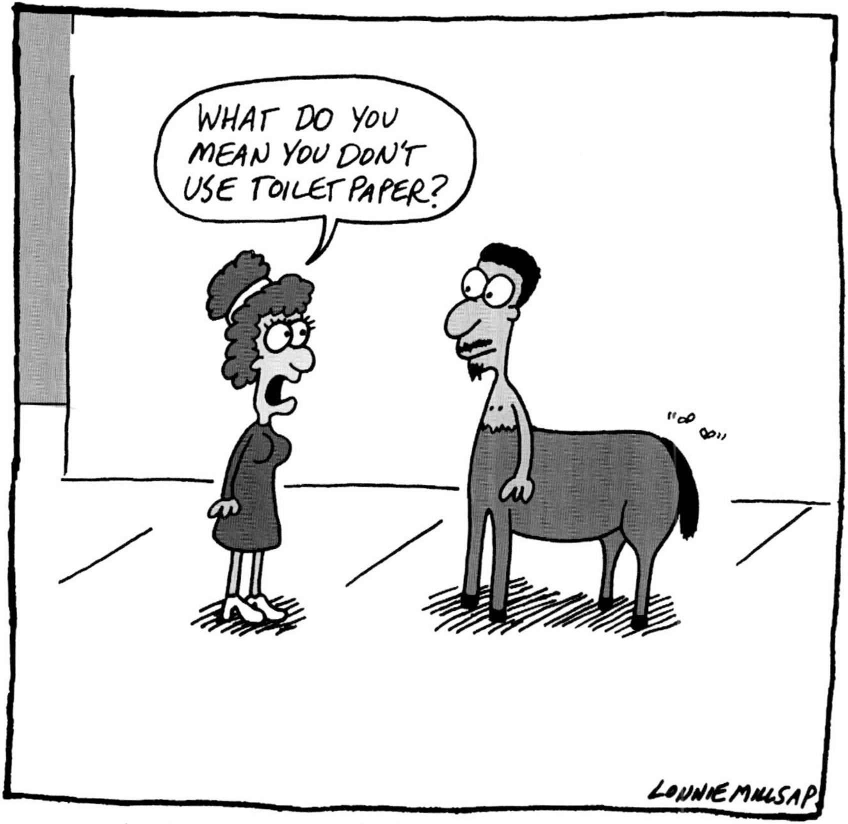
WHAT DO YOU MEAN YOU DON'T USE TOILET PAPER?
LONNIE MILLSAP

WHY CENTAURS DON'T GO ON MORE SECOND DATES

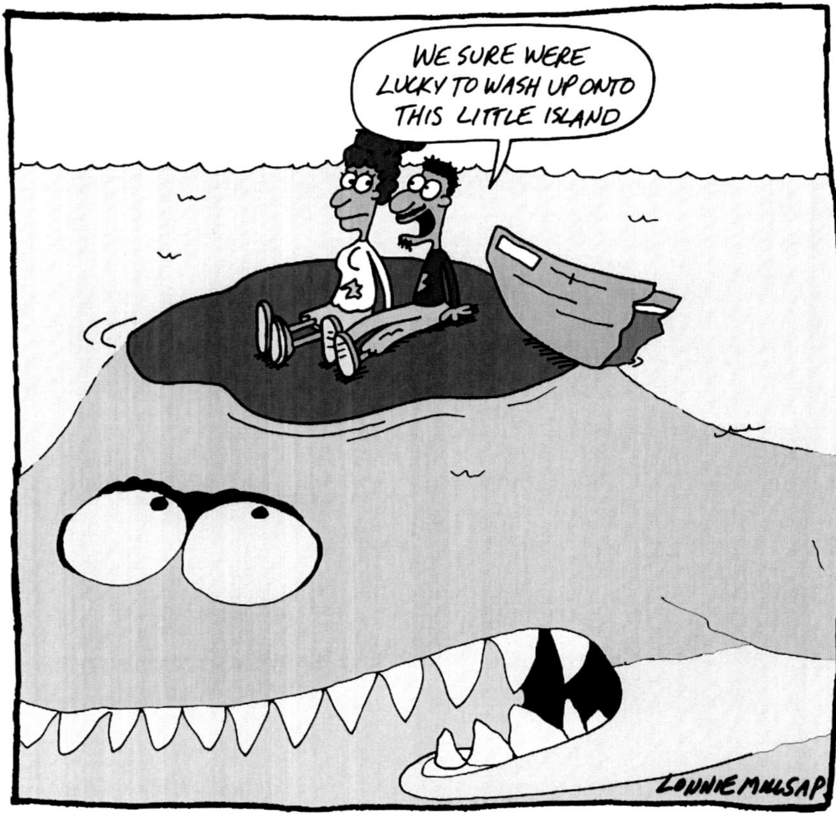
WE SURE WERE LUCKY TO WASH UP ONTO THIS LITTLE ISLAND
LONNIE MILLSAP

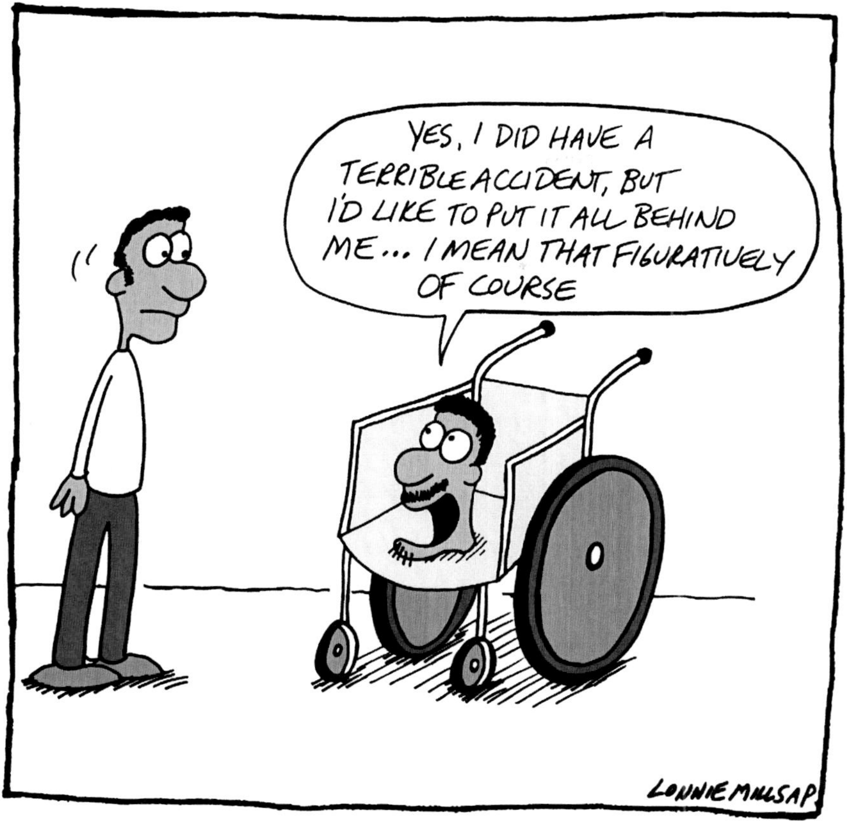
YES, I DID HAVE A TERRIBLE ACCIDENT, BUT I'D LIKE TO PUT IT ALL BEHIND ME... I MEAN THAT FIGURATIVELY OF COURSE
LONNIE MILLSAP

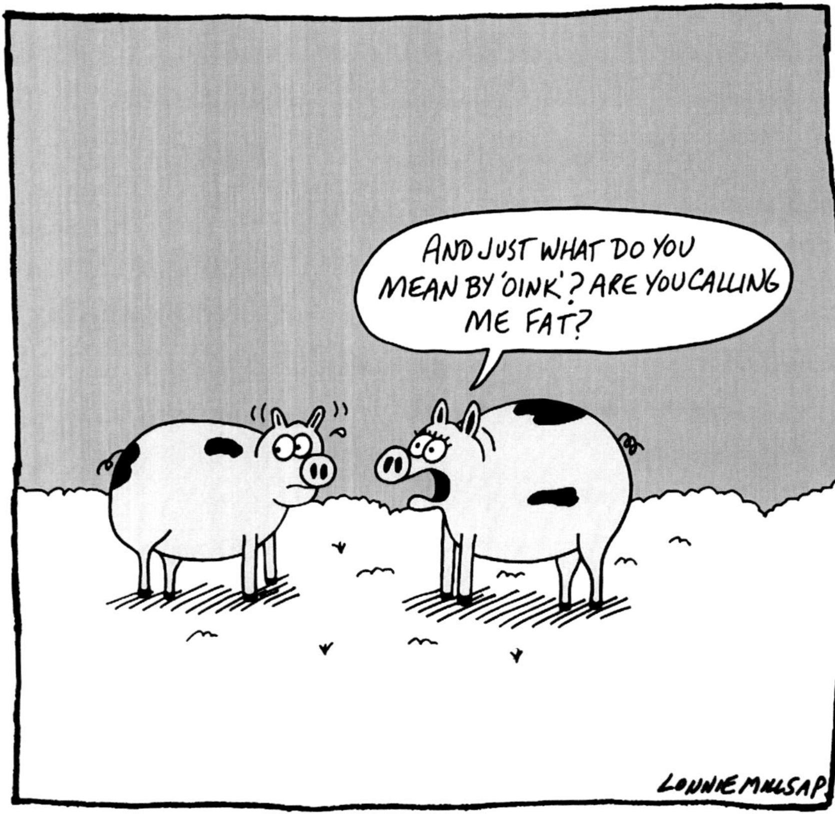
AND JUST WHAT DO YOU MEAN BY 'OINK'? ARE YOU CALLING ME FAT?
LONNIE MILLSAP

GUYS HAVE A HARD TIME THROUGHOUT THE ANIMAL KINGDOM

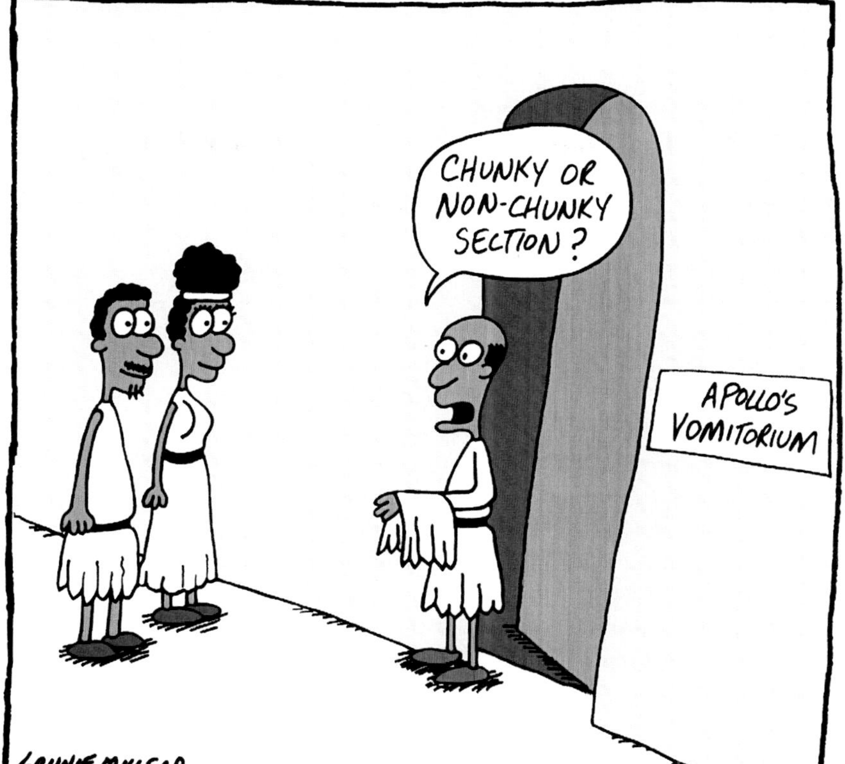
CHUNKY OR NON-CHUNKY SECTION?
APOLLO'S VOMITORIUM
LONNIE MILLSAP

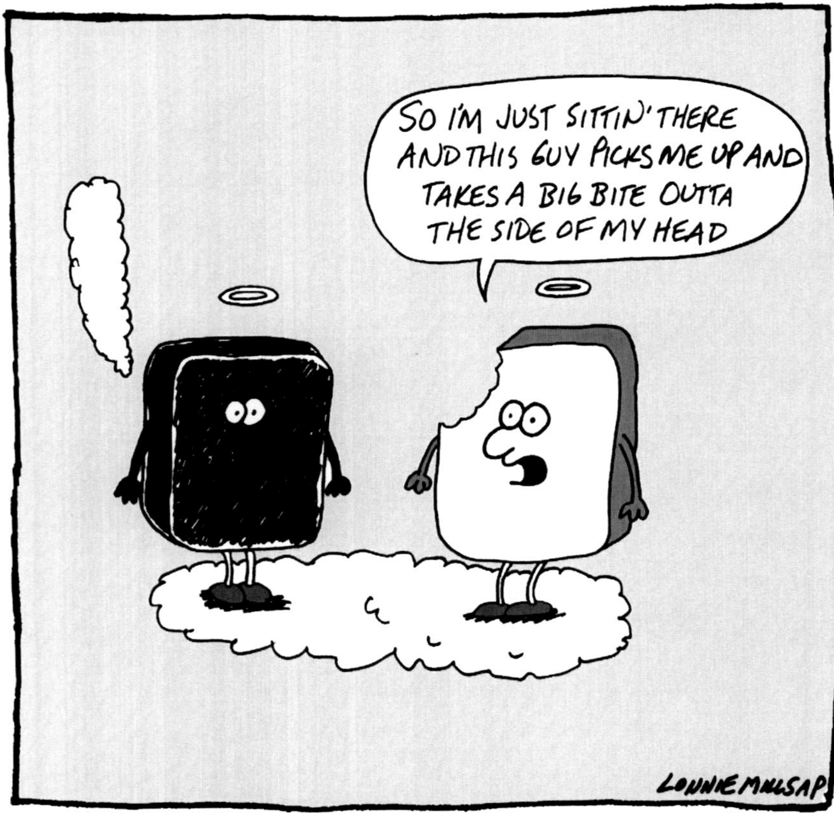
SO I'M JUST SITTIN' THERE AND THIS GUY PICKS ME UP AND TAKES A BIG BITE OUTTA THE SIDE OF MY HEAD
LONNIE MILLSAP

SWAPPING STORIES IN TOAST HEAVEN

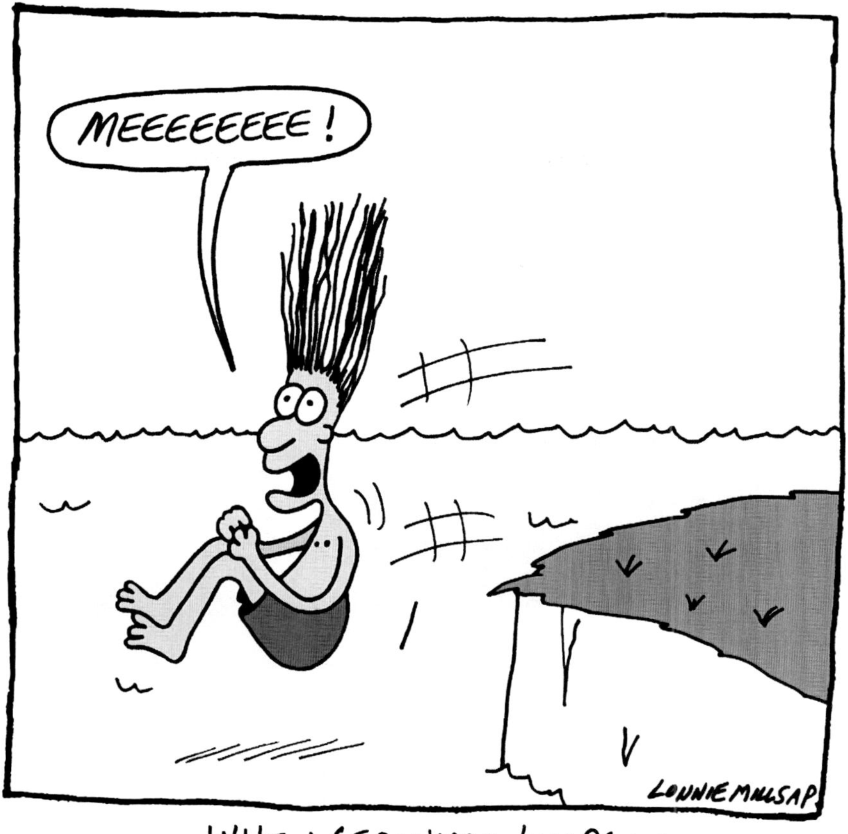
MEEEEEEEEE!
LONNIE MILLSAP

WHEN GERONIMO JUMPS IN

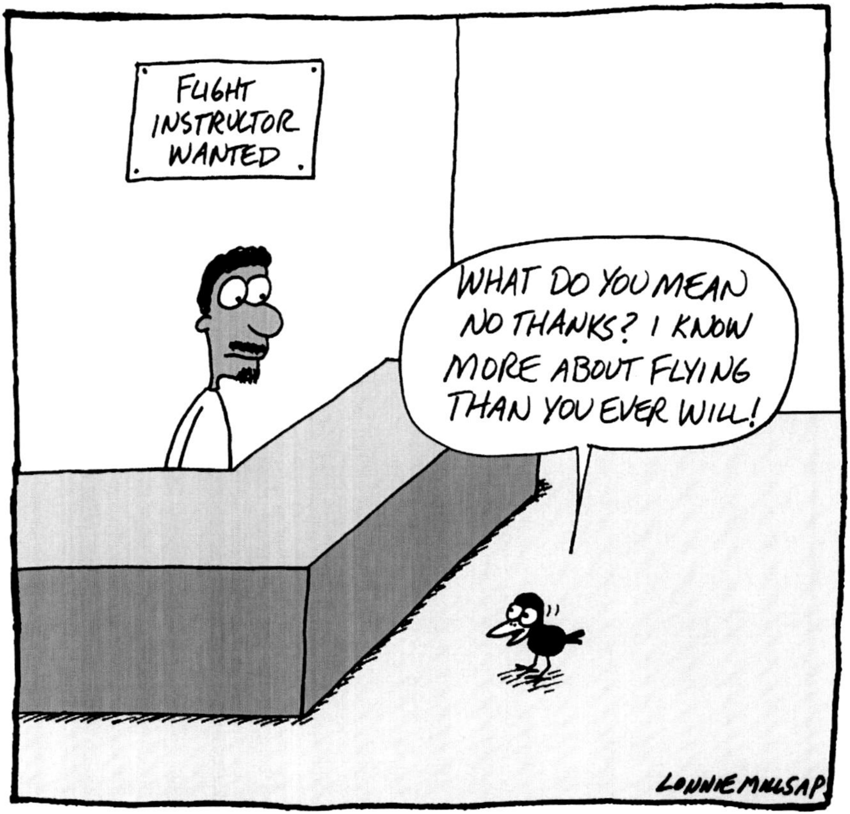
FLIGHT INSTRUCTOR WANTED
WHAT DO YOU MEAN NO THANKS? I KNOW MORE ABOUT FLYING THAN YOU EVER WILL!
LONNIE MILLSAP

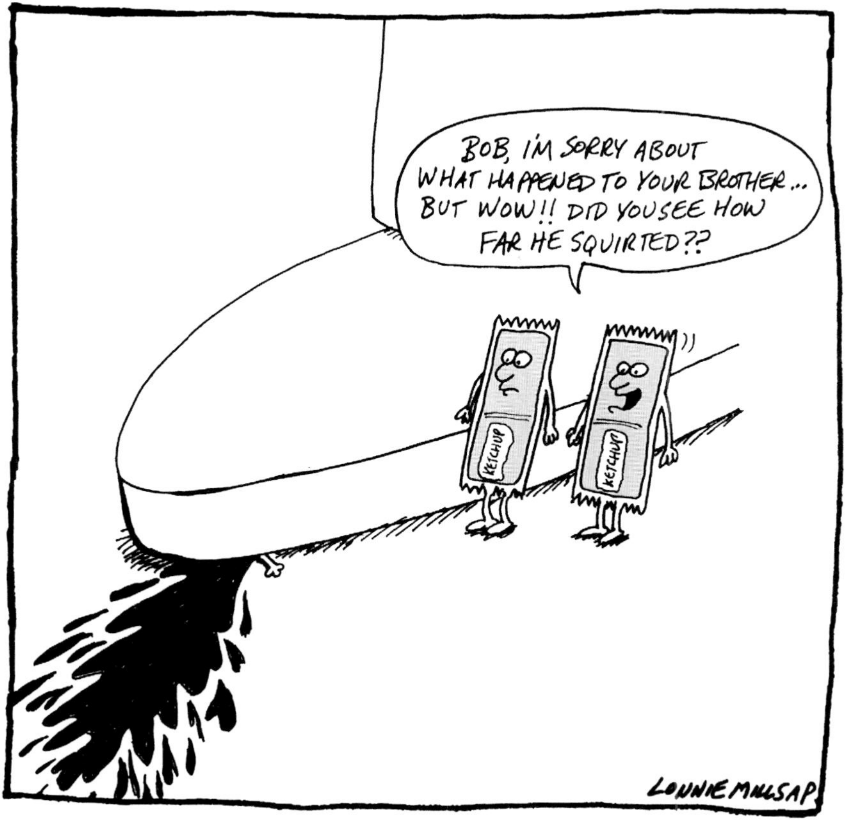
BOB, I'M SORRY ABOUT WHAT HAPPENED TO YOUR BROTHER... BUT WOW!! DID YOU SEE HOW FAR HE SQUIRTED??
KETCHUP
KETCHUP
LONNIE MILLSAP

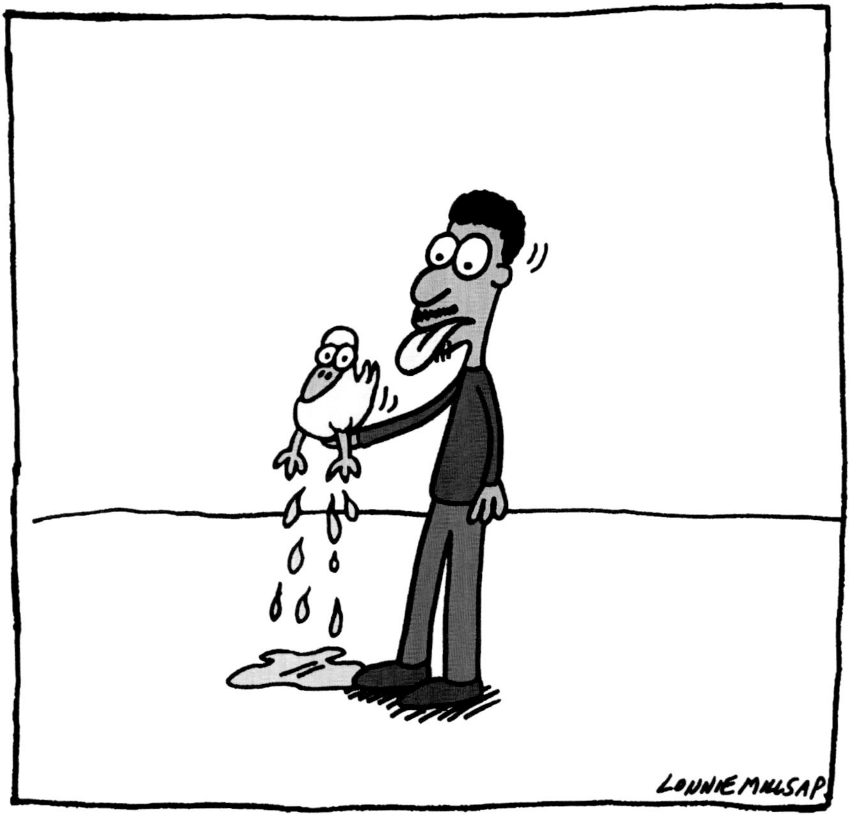
LONNIE MILLSAP

BOB WOULD RATHER HAVE TWO BIRDS IN THE BUSH

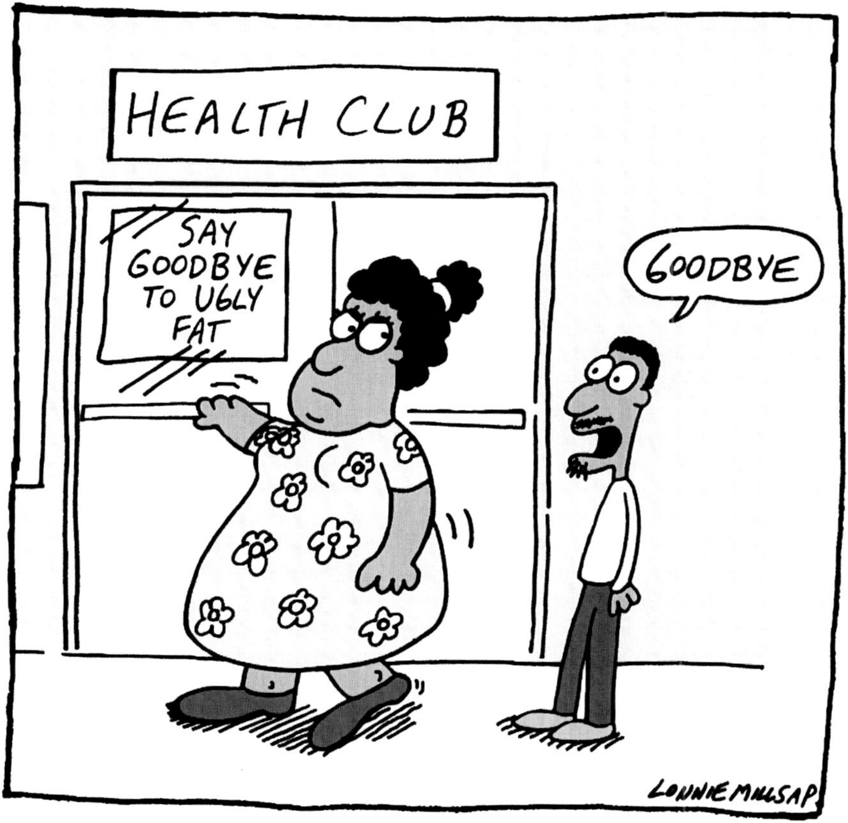
HEALTH CLUB
SAY GOODBYE TO UGLY FAT
GOODBYE
LONNIE MILLSAP

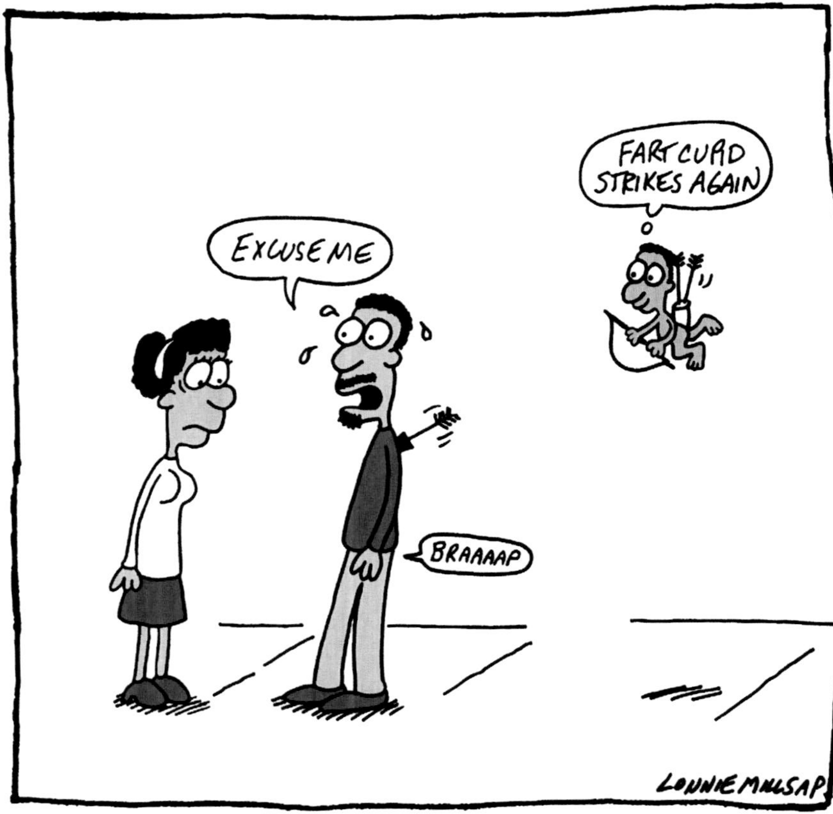
EXCUSE ME
BRAAAAP
FART CUPID STRIKES AGAIN
LONNIE MILLSAP

THAT OTHER CUPID THAT NO ONE REALLY KNOWS ABOUT

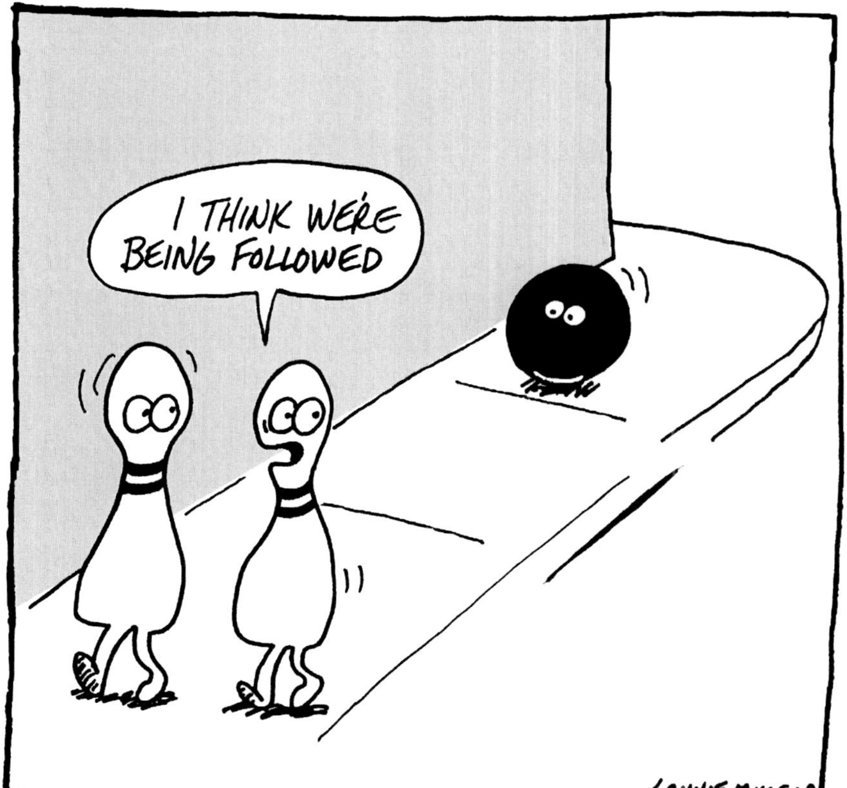
I THINK WE'RE BEING FOLLOWED
LONNIE MILLSAP

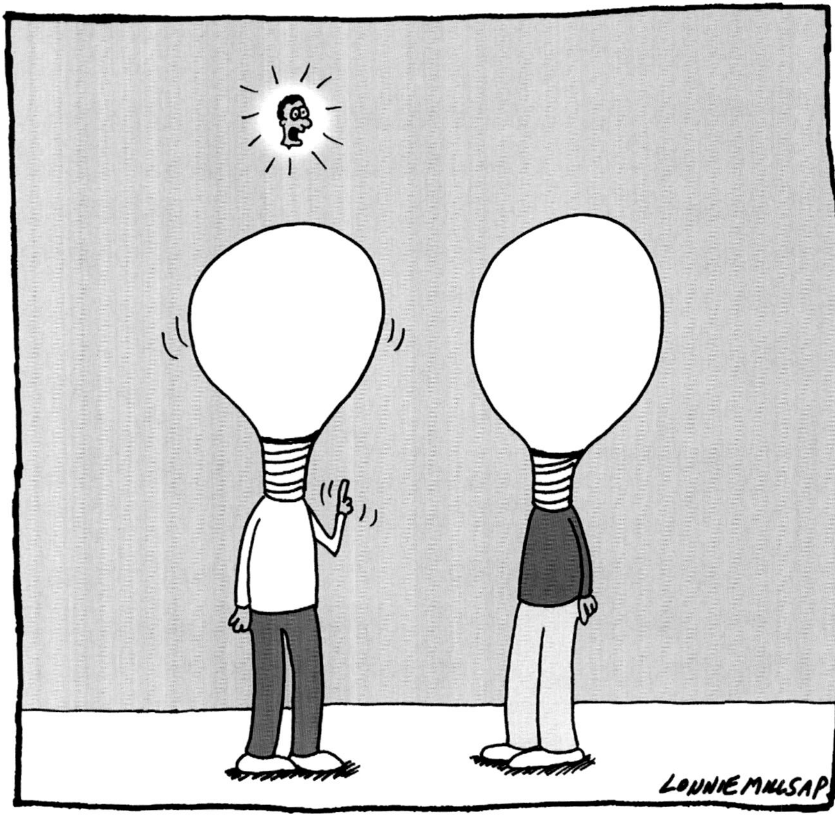
LONNIE MILLSAP

WHEN LIGHT BULBS HAVE AN IDEA

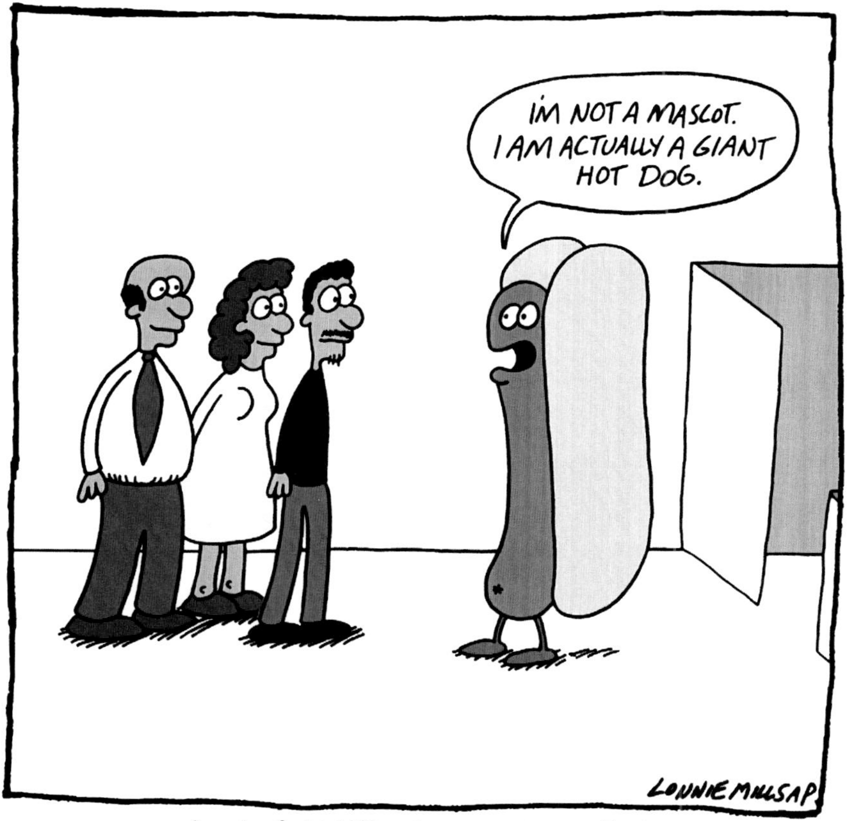
I'M NOT A MASCOT. I AM ACTUALLY A GIANT HOT DOG.
LONNIE MILLSAP

AN HOUR LATER, AT LUNCHTIME, RANDY REGRETTED CONFIDING TO HIS CO-WORKERS

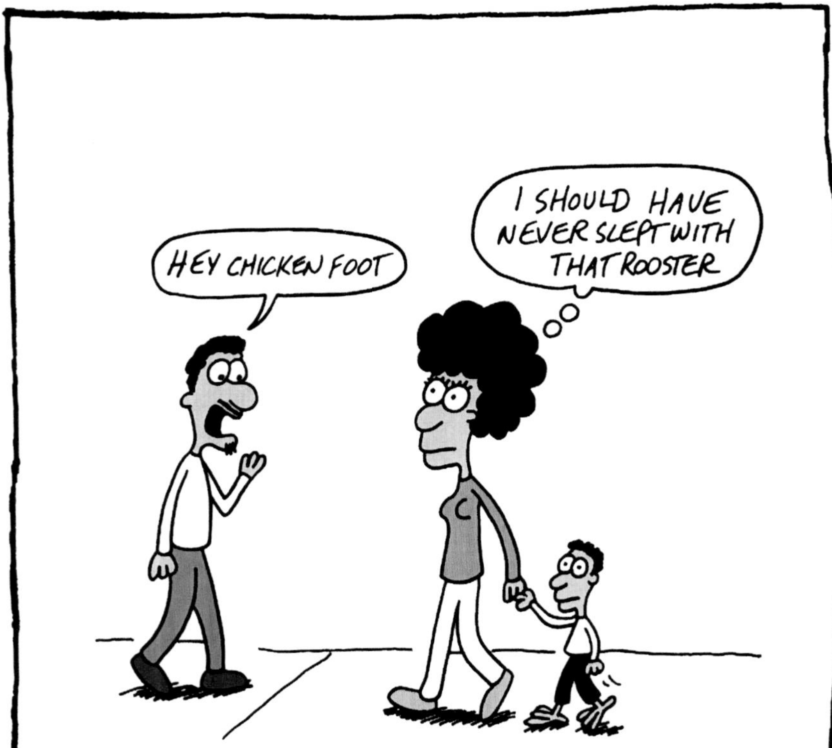
HEY CHICKEN FOOT
I SHOULD HAVE NEVER SLEPT WITH THAT ROOSTER
LONNIE MILLSAP

CROSS SPECIES DATING REGRETS

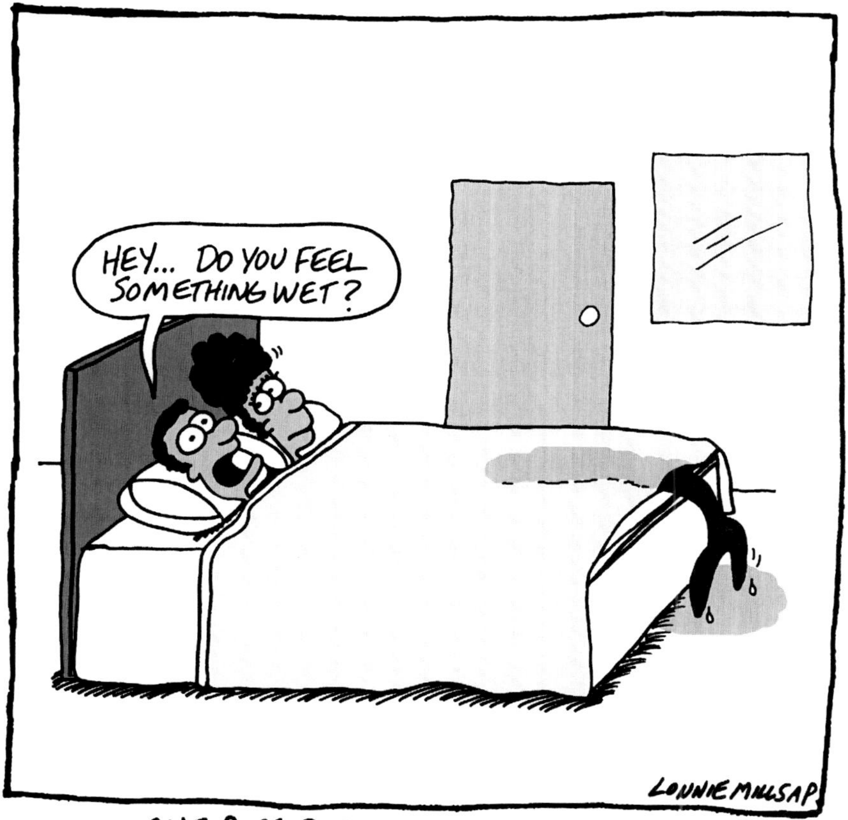
HEY... DO YOU FEEL SOMETHING WET?
LONNIE MILLSAP

ONE POSSIBLE DRAWBACK OF HAVING A ONE NIGHT STAND WITH A MERMAID

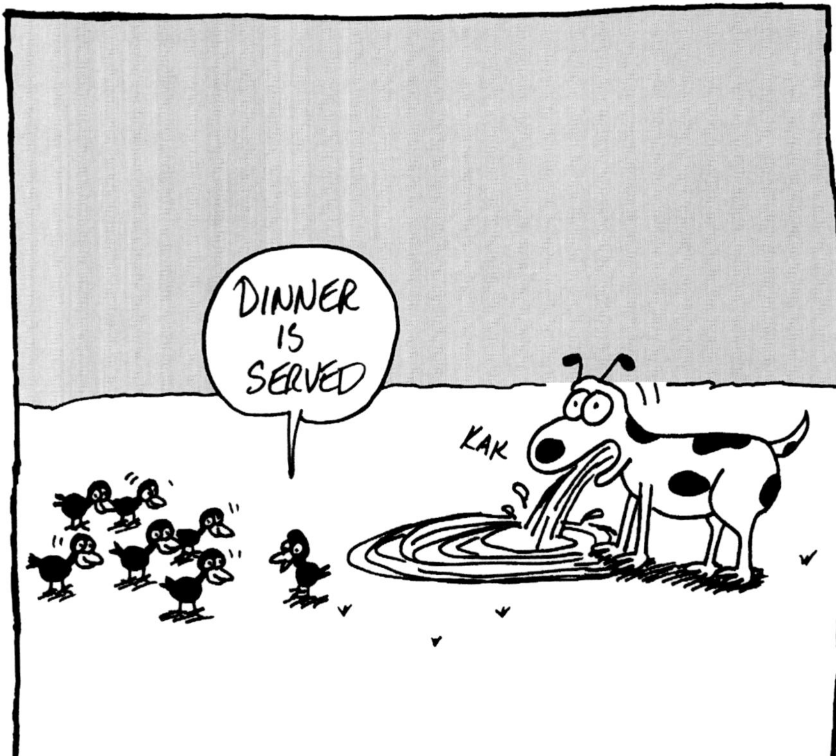
DINNER IS SERVED
KAK
LONNIE MILLSAP

A BLACKBIRD FAMILY THANKSGIVING

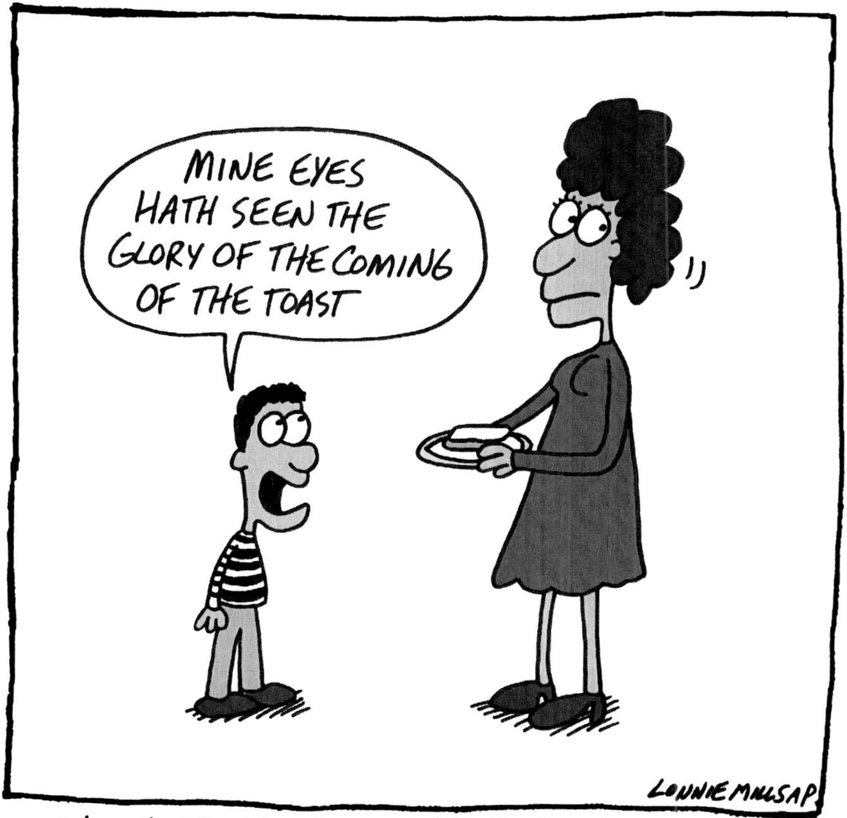
MINE EYES HATH SEEN THE GLORY OF THE COMING OF THE TOAST
LONNIE MILLSAP

YOUNG MARTIN LUTHER KING AT BREAKFAST

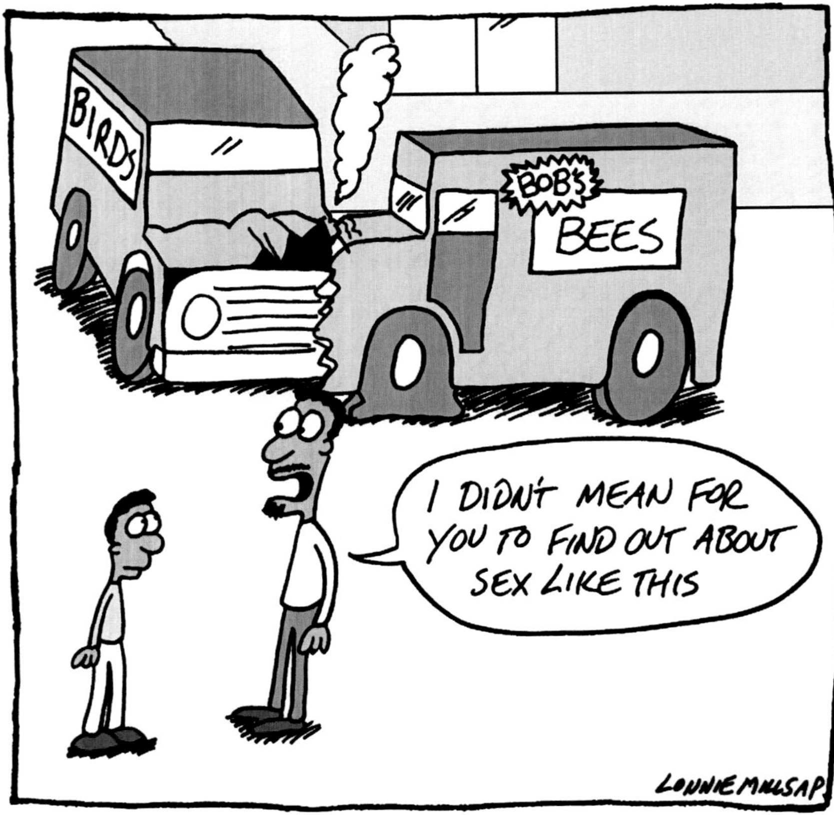
BIRDS
BOB'S
BEES
I DIDN'T MEAN FOR YOU TO FIND OUT ABOUT SEX LIKE THIS
LONNIE MILLSAP

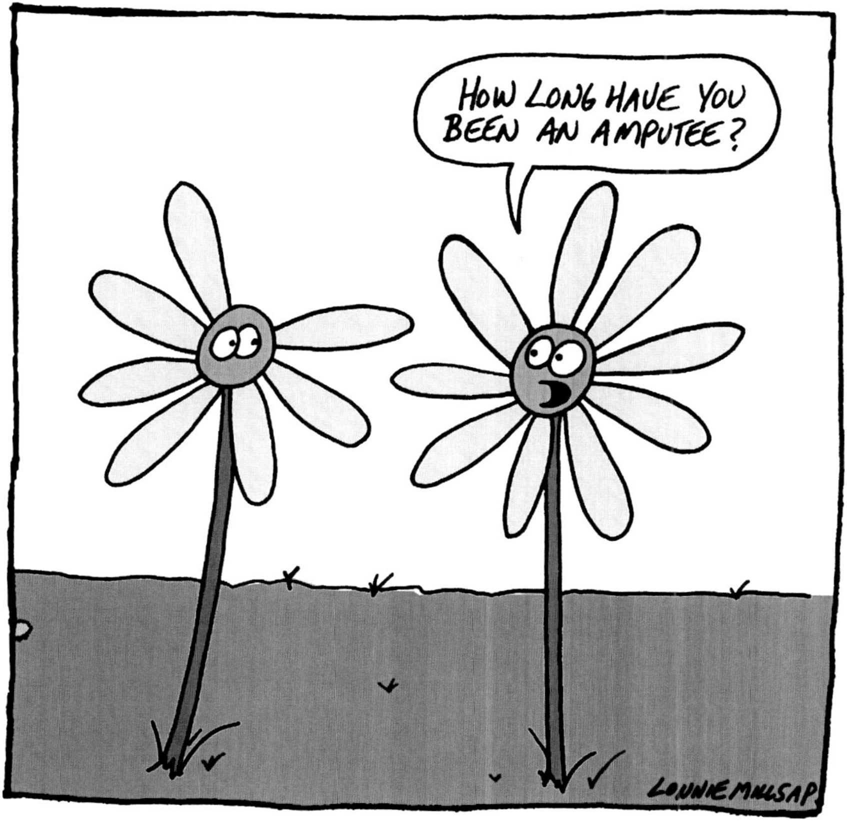
HOW LONG HAVE YOU BEEN AN AMPUTEE?
LONNIE MILLSAP

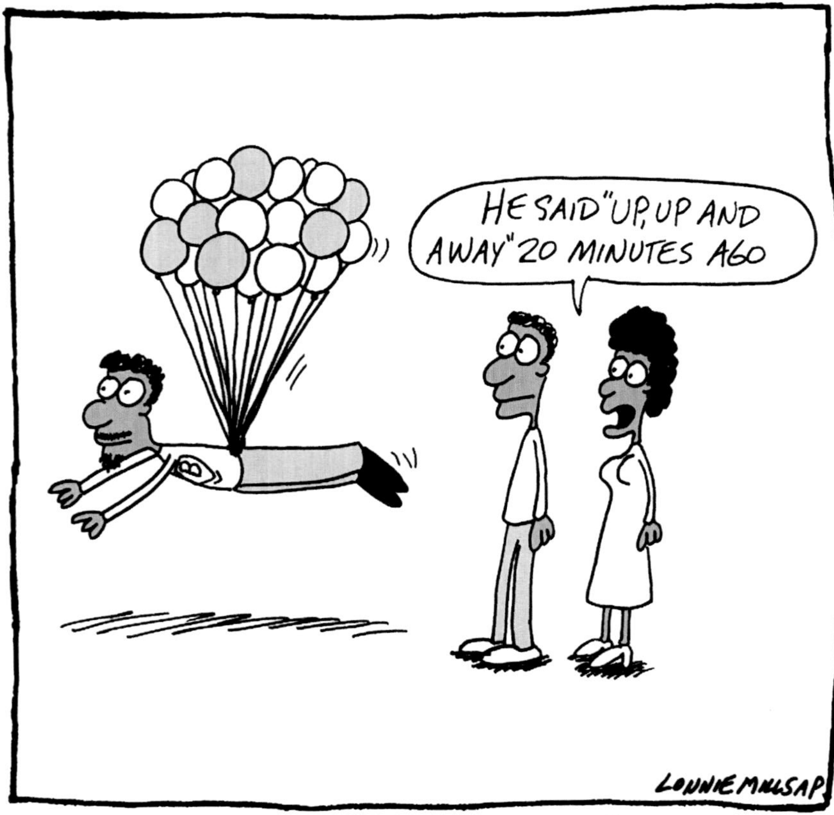
HE SAID "UP, UP AND AWAY" 20 MINUTES AGO
LONNIE MILLSAP

THE MORTALITY RATE FOR WHOMEVER BALLOONMAN TRIES TO RESCUE IS PRETTY HIGH

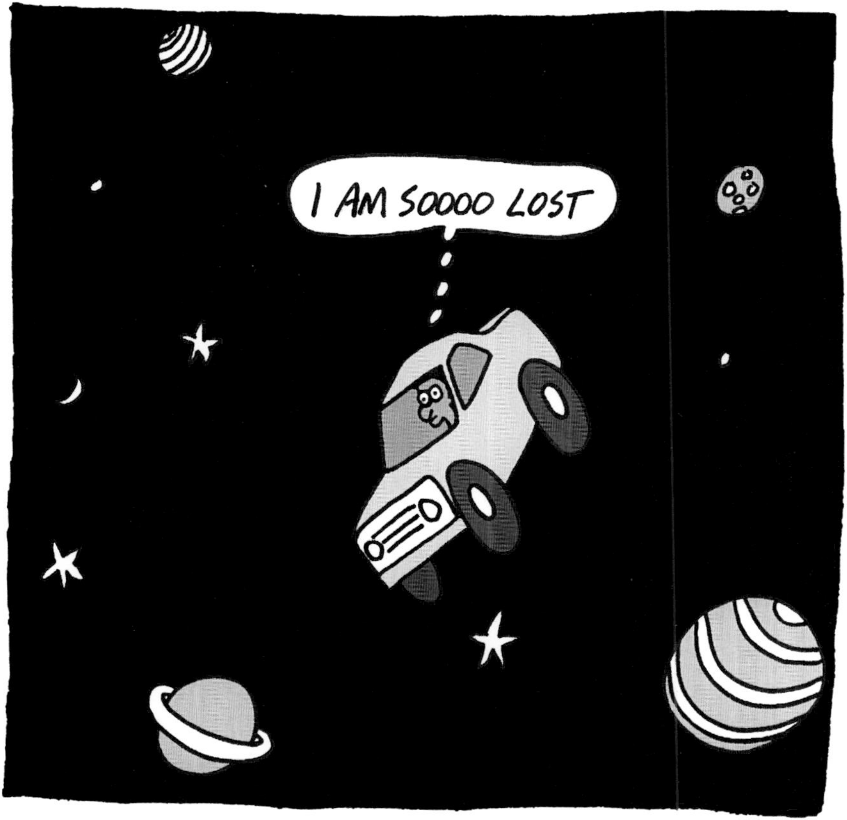
I AM SOOOO LOST

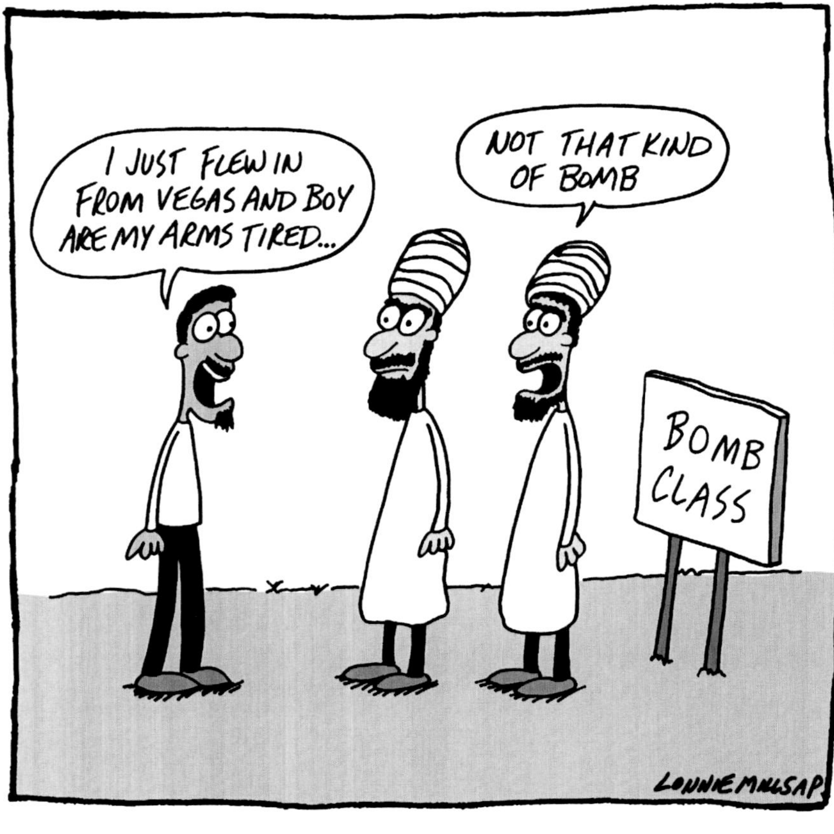
I JUST FLEW IN FROM VEGAS AND BOY ARE MY ARMS TIRED...
NOT THAT KIND OF BOMB
BOMB CLASS
LONNIE MILLSAP

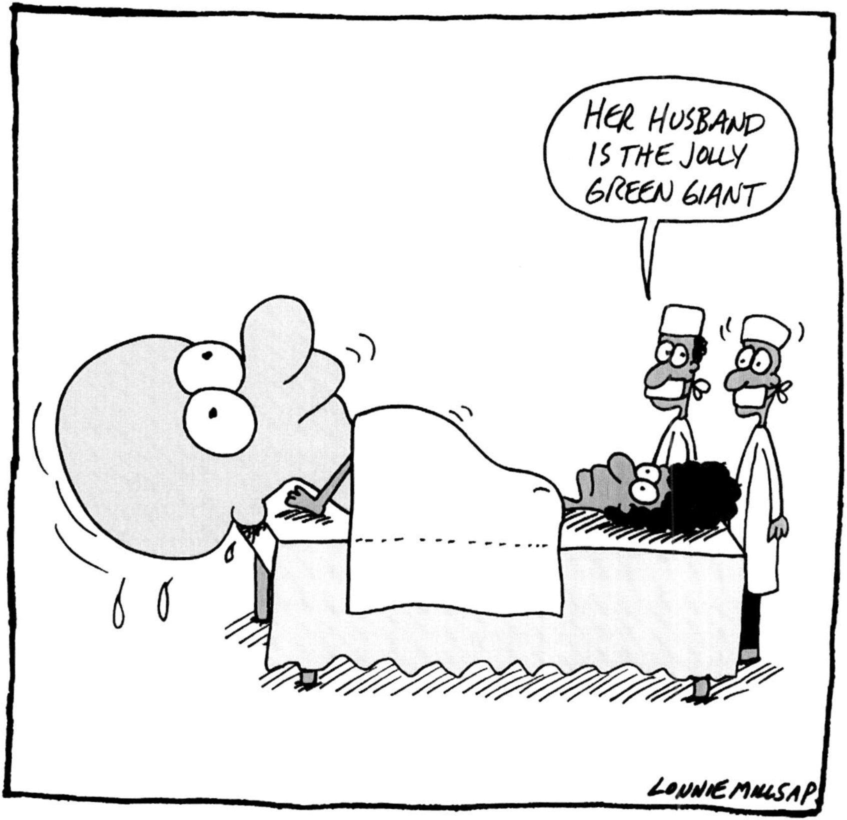
HER HUSBAND IS THE JOLLY GREEN GIANT
LONNIE MILLSAP

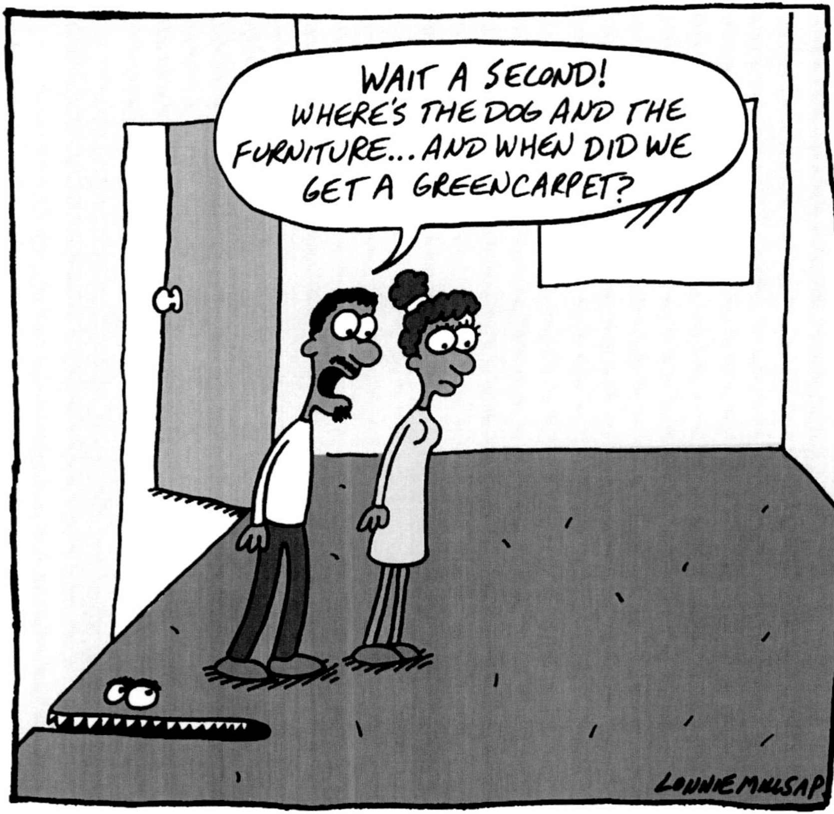
WAIT A SECOND! WHERE'S THE DOG AND THE FURNITURE... AND WHEN DID WE GET A GREENCARPET?
LONNIE MILLSAP

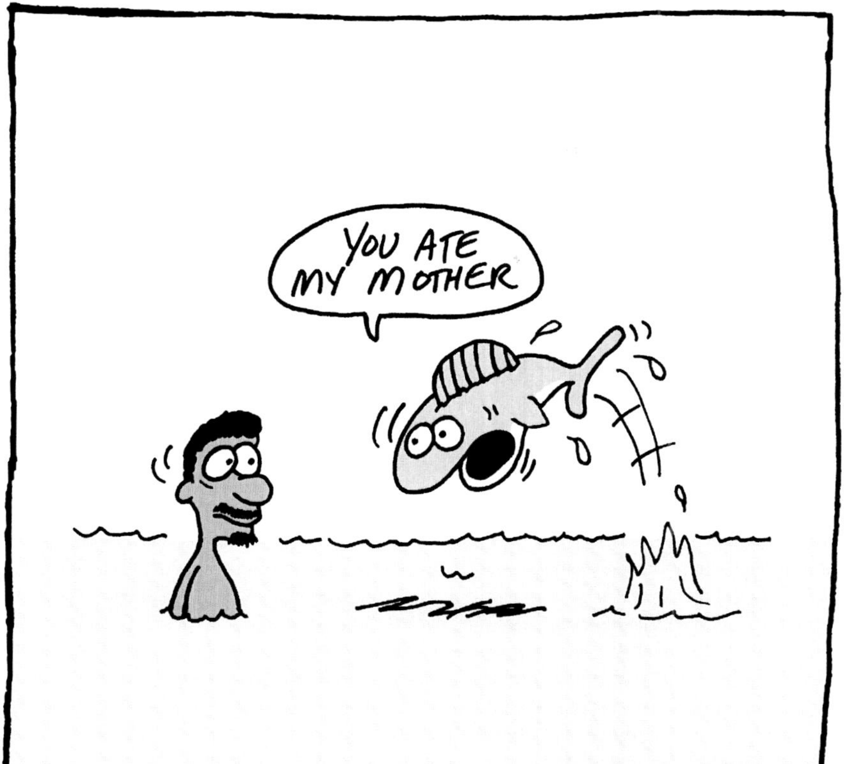
YOU ATE MY MOTHER
LONNIE MILLSAP

THE RARELY SEEN GUILTFISH

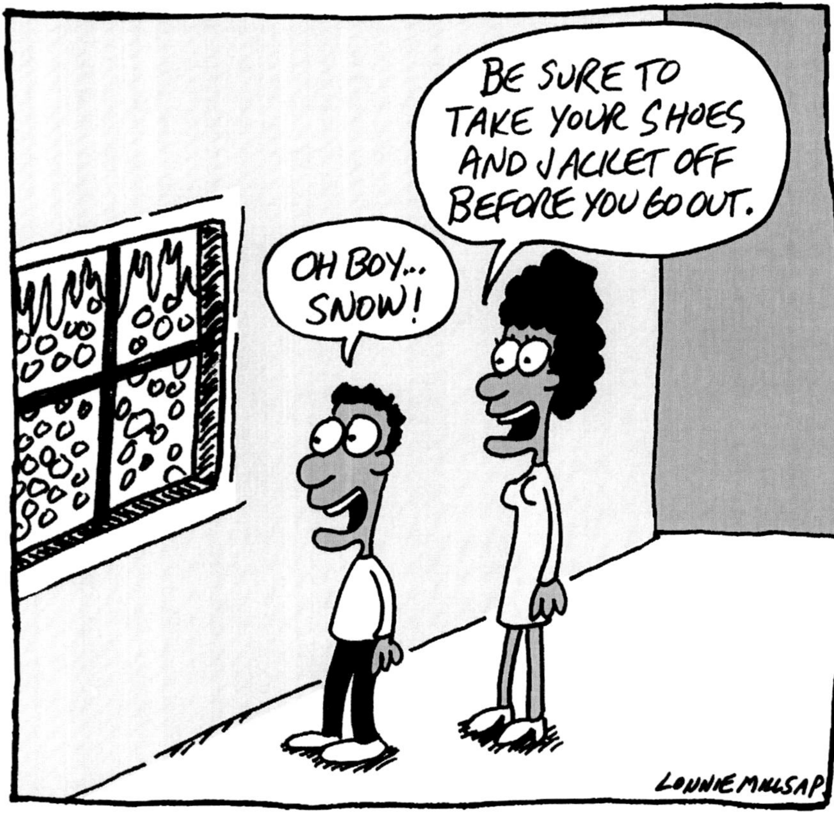
OH BOY... SNOW!
BE SURE TO TAKE YOUR SHOES AND JACKET OFF BEFORE YOU GO OUT.
LONNIE MILLSAP

WHEN PARENTS NEED EXTRA SPACE

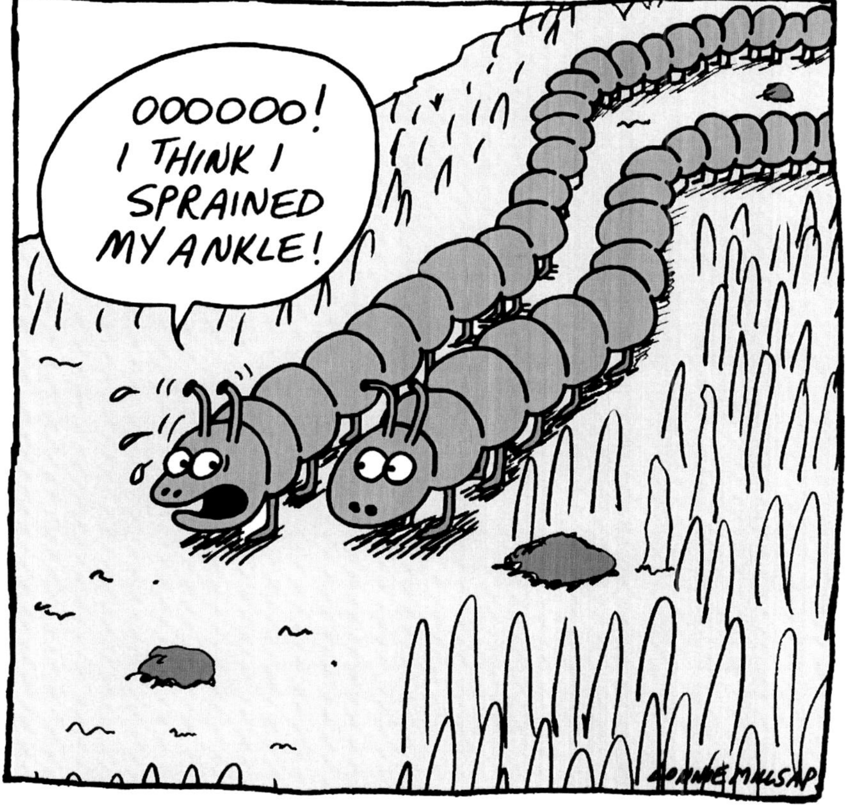
OOOOOO! I THINK I SPRAINED MY ANKLE!

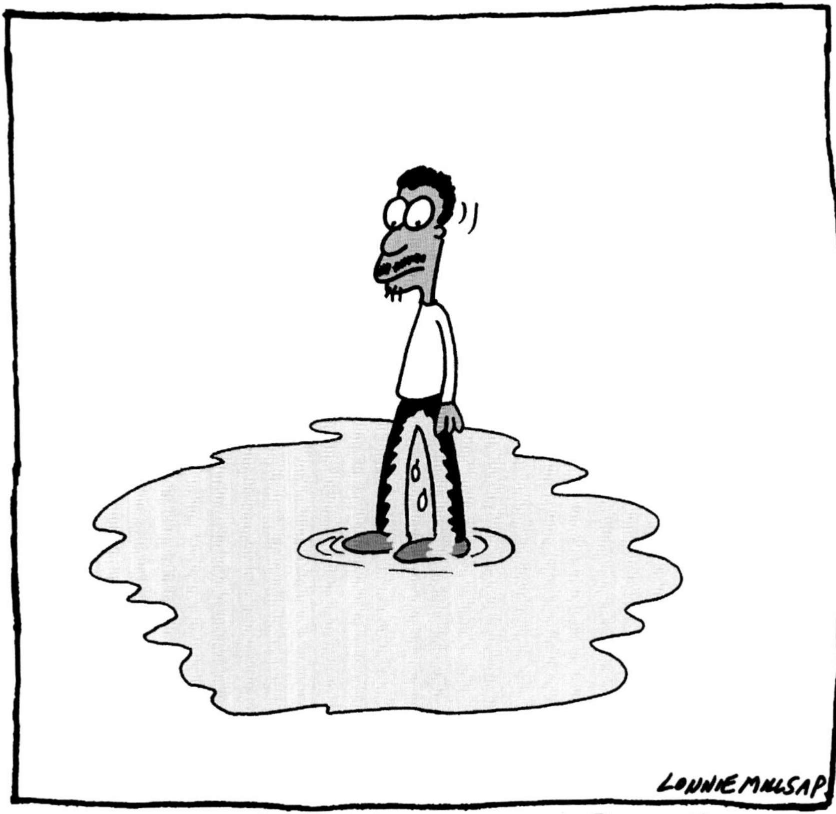
LONNIE MILLSAP

THE WORLD'S FIRST ELEPHANT BLADDER TRANSPLANT RECIPIENT ACCIDENT

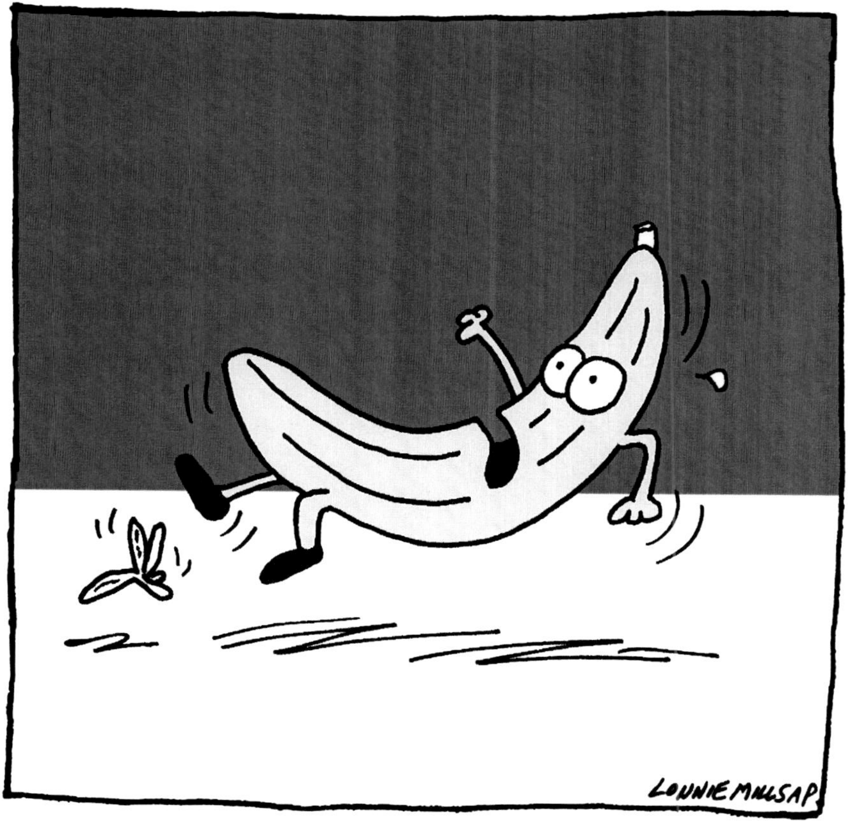
LONNIE MILLSAP

IRONY ON PLANET BANANA

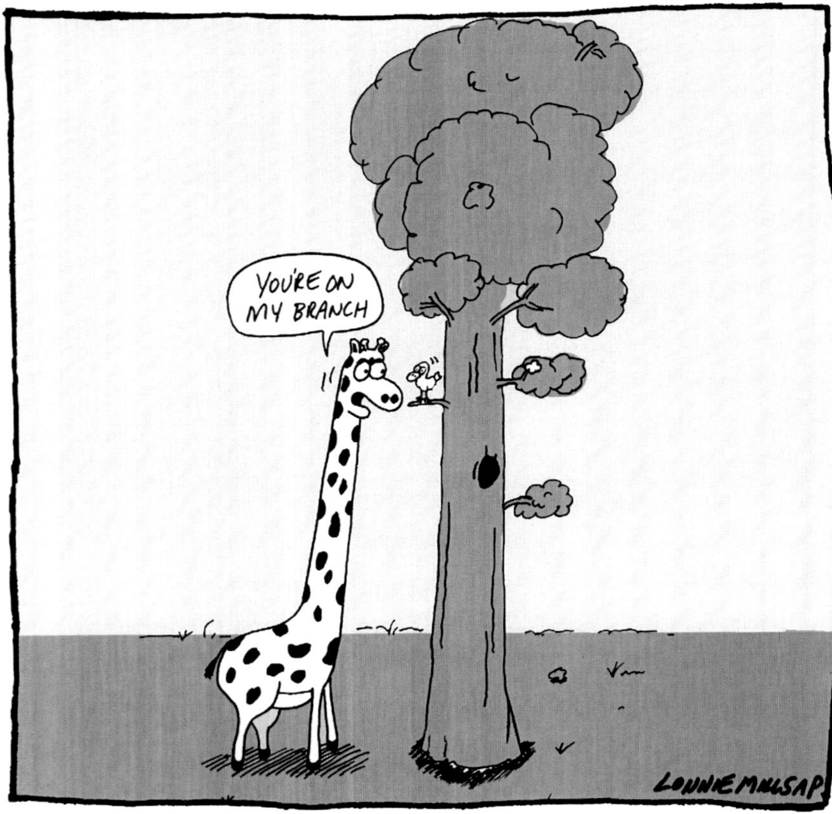
YOU'RE ON MY BRANCH
LONNIE MILLSAP

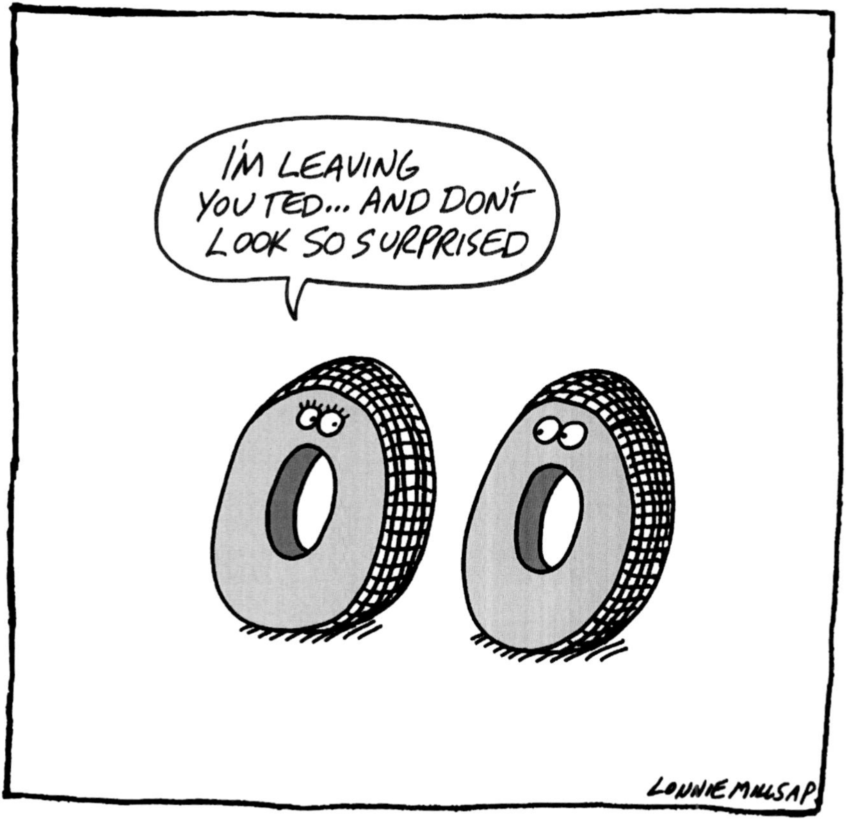
I'M LEAVING YOU TED... AND DON'T LOOK SO SURPRISED
LONNIE MILLSAP

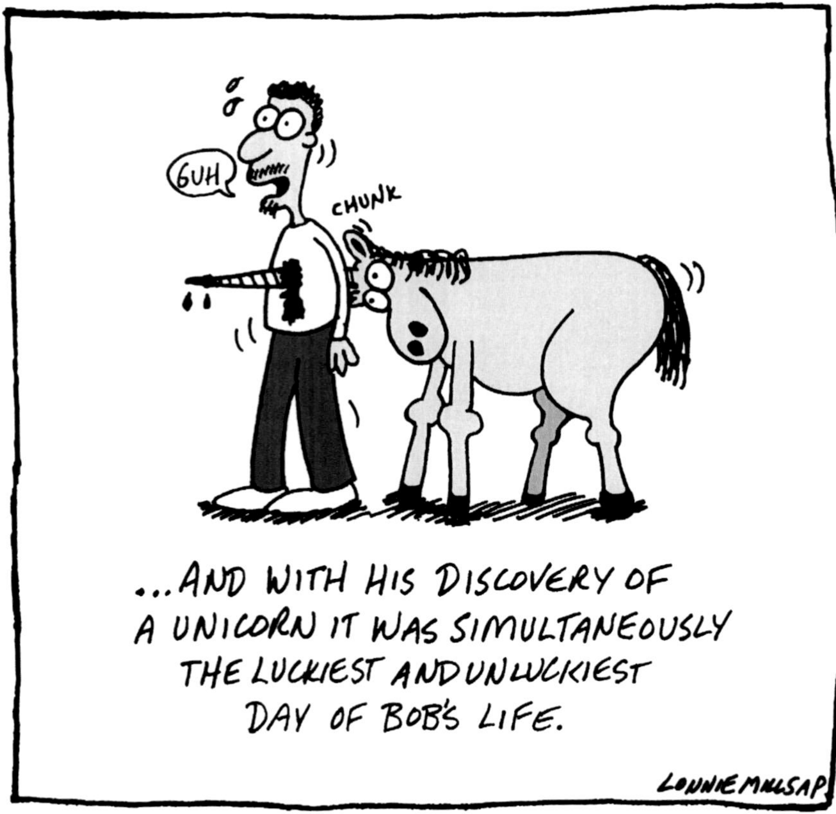
GUH
CHUNK
LONNIE MILLSAP

...AND WITH HIS DISCOVERY OF A UNICORN IT WAS SIMULTANEOUSLY THE LUCKIEST AND UNLUCKIEST DAY OF BOB'S LIFE.

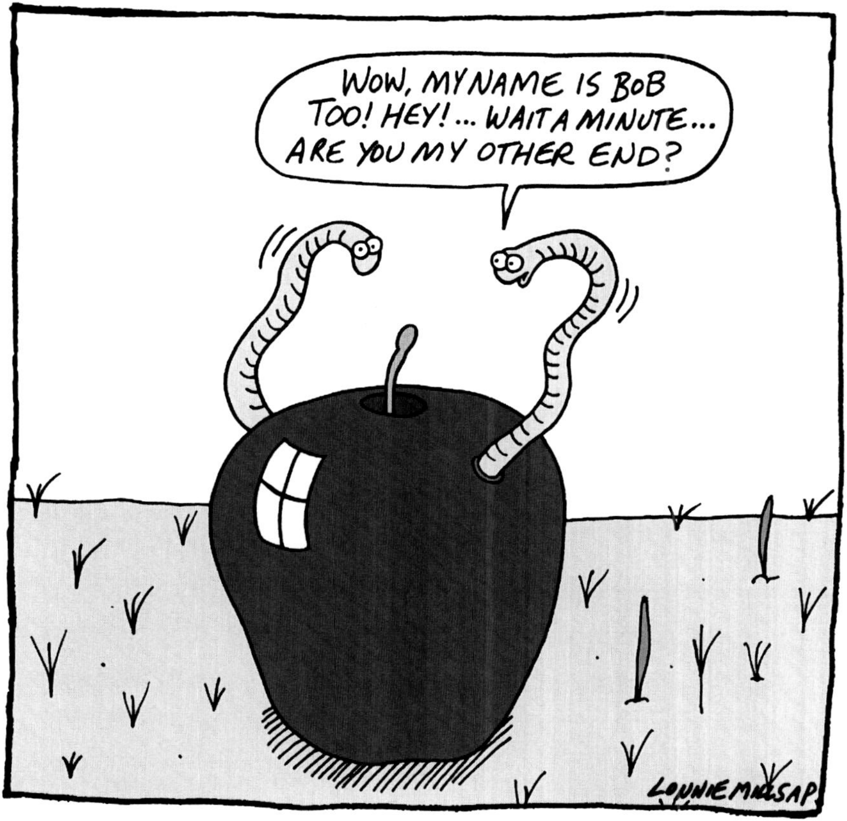
WOW, MY NAME IS BOB TOO! HEY! ... WAIT A MINUTE... ARE YOU MY OTHER END?
LONNIE MILLSAP

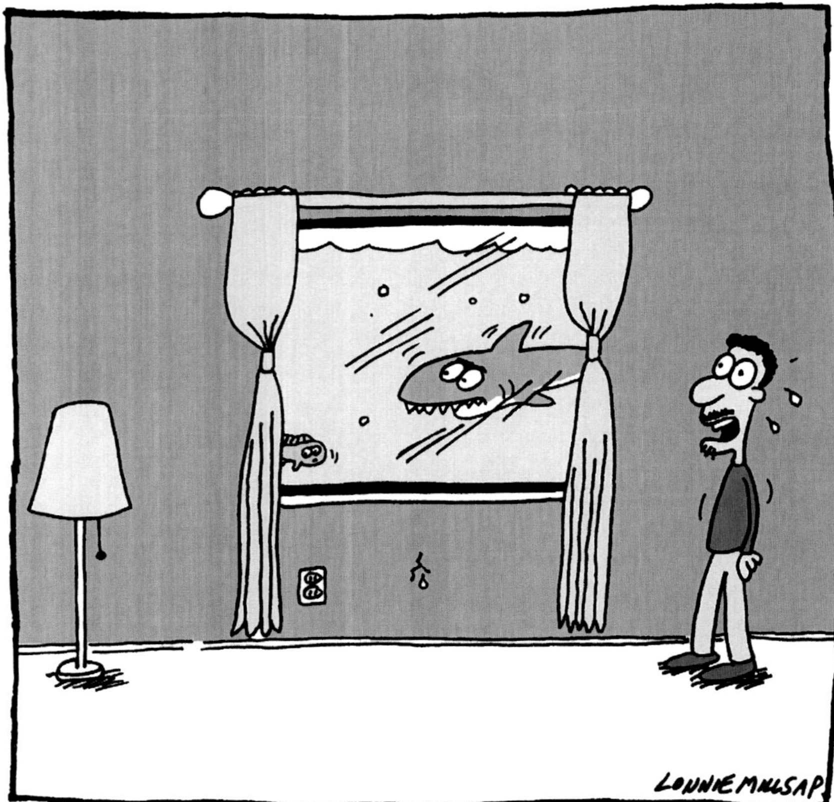
LONNIE MILLSAP

THE ABSOLUTE WORST THING YOU CAN SEE THROUGH YOUR 86TH STORY APARTMENT WINDOW

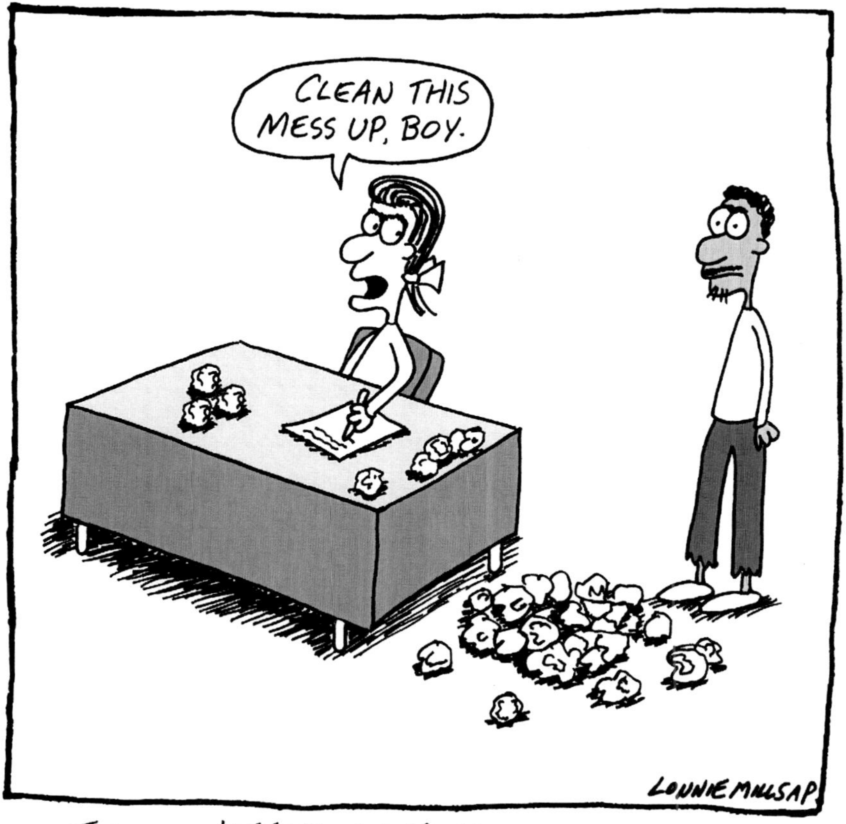
CLEAN THIS MESS UP, BOY.
LONNIE MILLSAP

THOMAS JEFFERSON DURING EARLY DRAFTS OF THE DECLARATION OF INDEPENDENCE

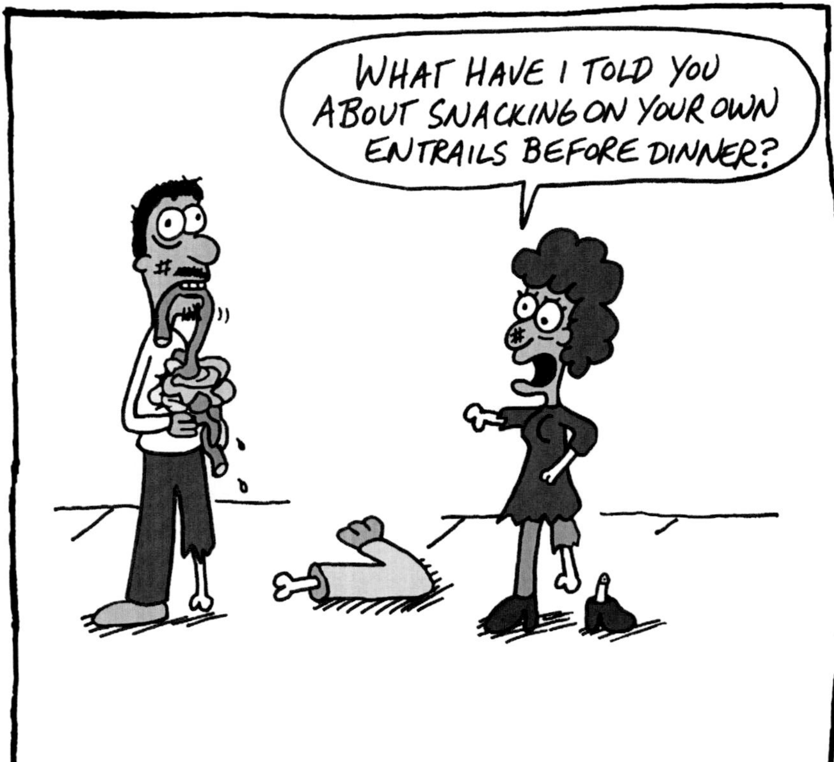
WHAT HAVE I TOLD YOU ABOUT SNACKING ON YOUR OWN ENTRAILS BEFORE DINNER?
LONNIE MILLSAP

A MOTHER ZOMBIE'S WORK IS NEVER FINISHED

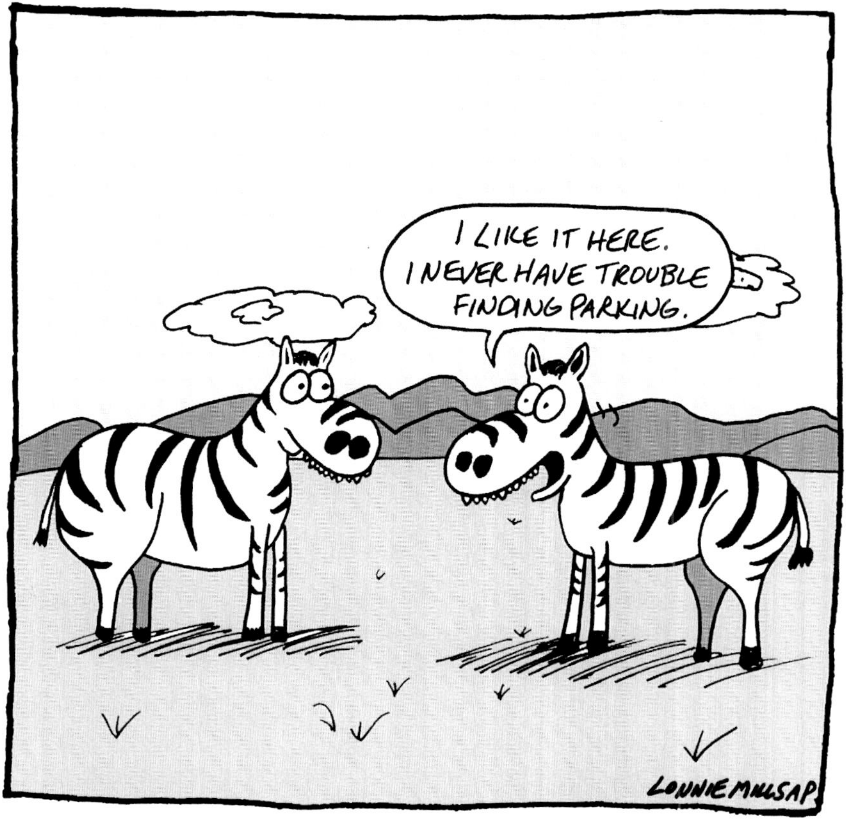
I LIKE IT HERE. I NEVER HAVE TROUBLE FINDING PARKING.
LONNIE MILLSAP

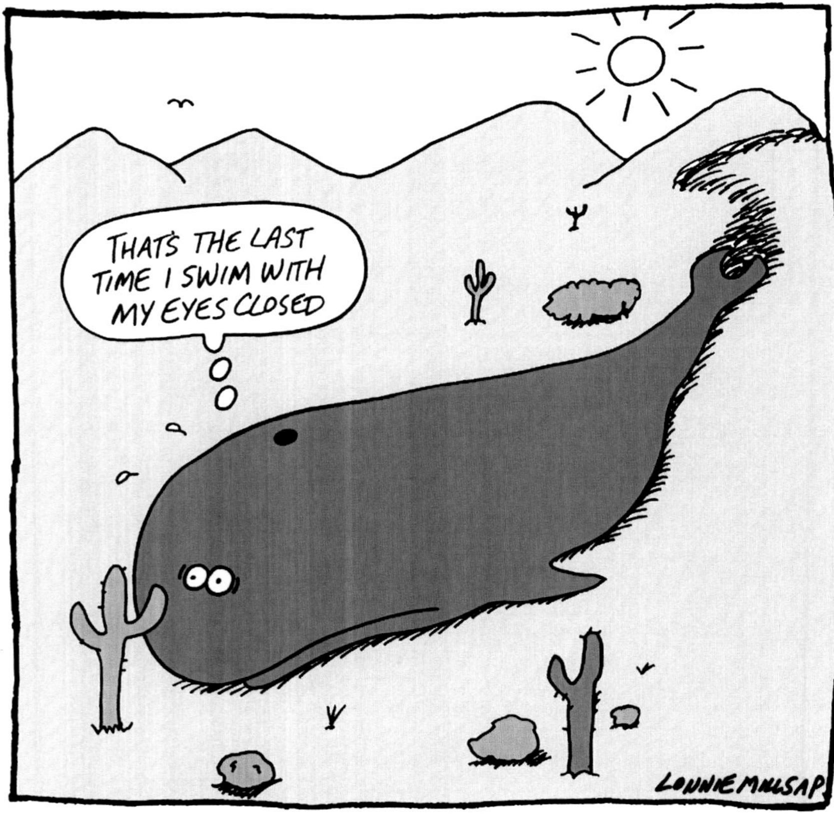
THAT'S THE LAST TIME I SWIM WITH MY EYES CLOSED
LONNIE MILLSAP

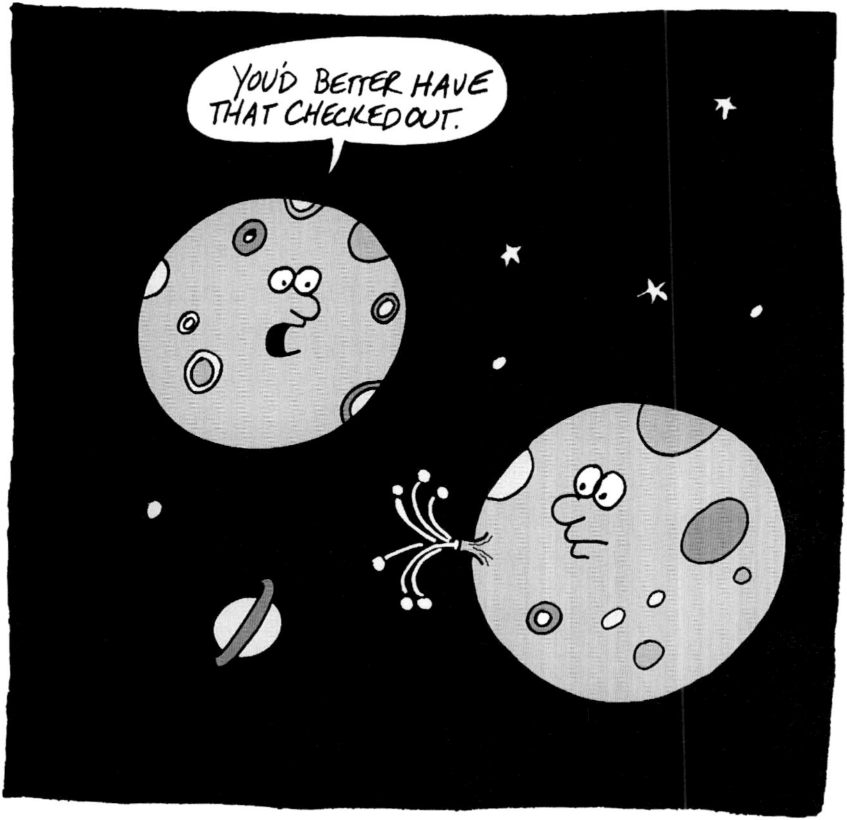
YOU'D BETTER HAVE THAT CHECKED OUT.

IF PLANETS COULD TALK

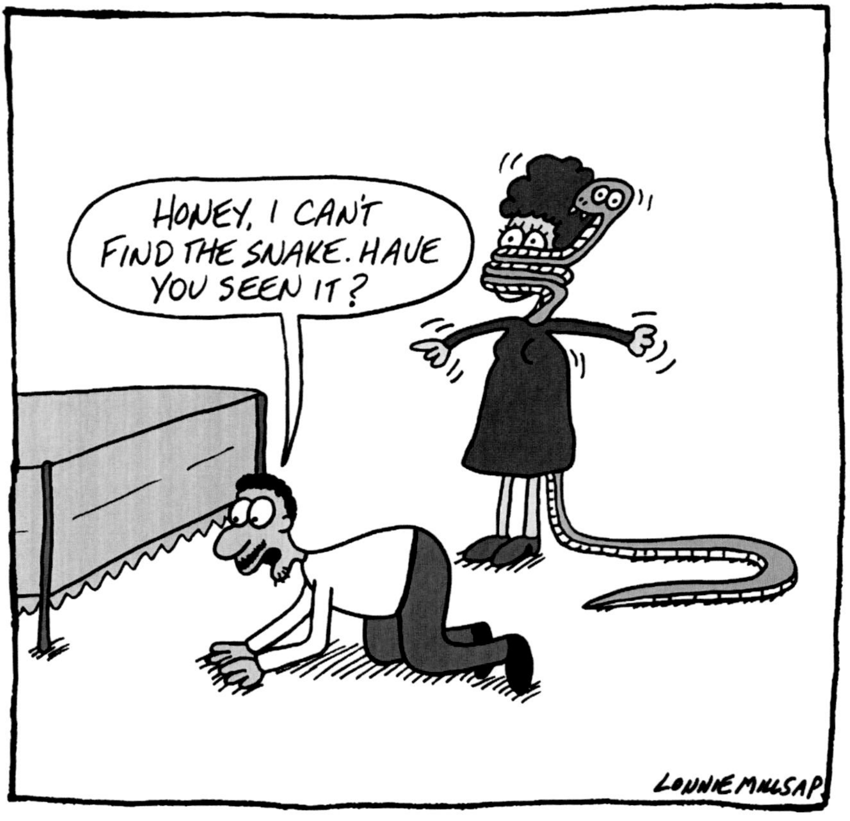
HONEY, I CAN'T FIND THE SNAKE. HAVE YOU SEEN IT?
LONNIE MILLSAP

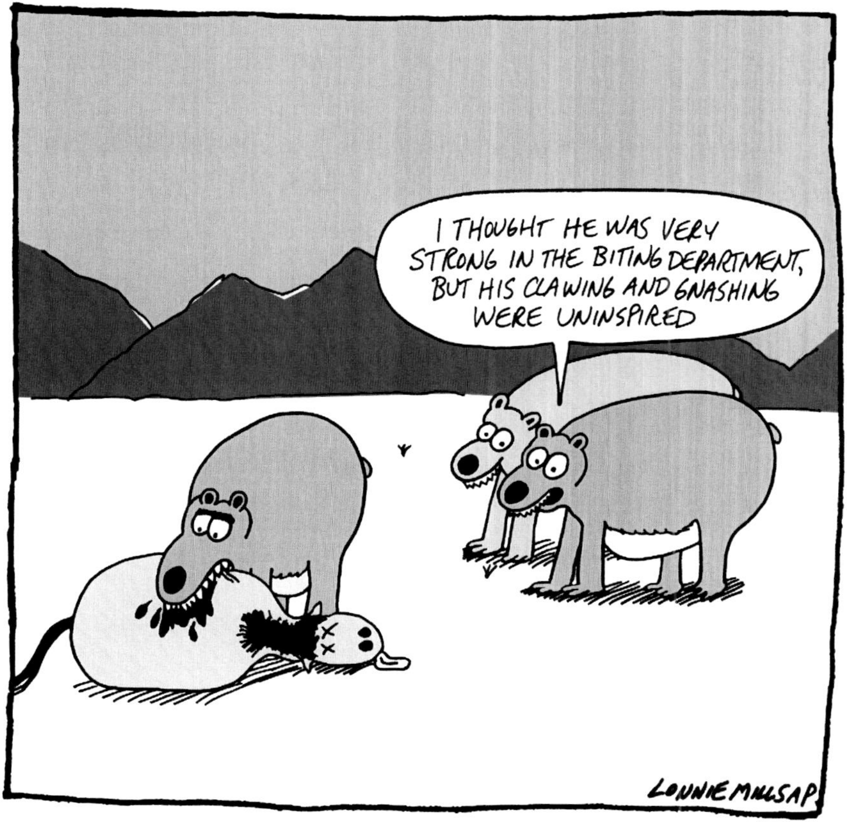
I THOUGHT HE WAS VERY STRONG IN THE BITING DEPARTMENT, BUT HIS CLAWING AND GNASHING WERE UNINSPIRED
LONNIE MILLSAP

ANIMAL CRITICS

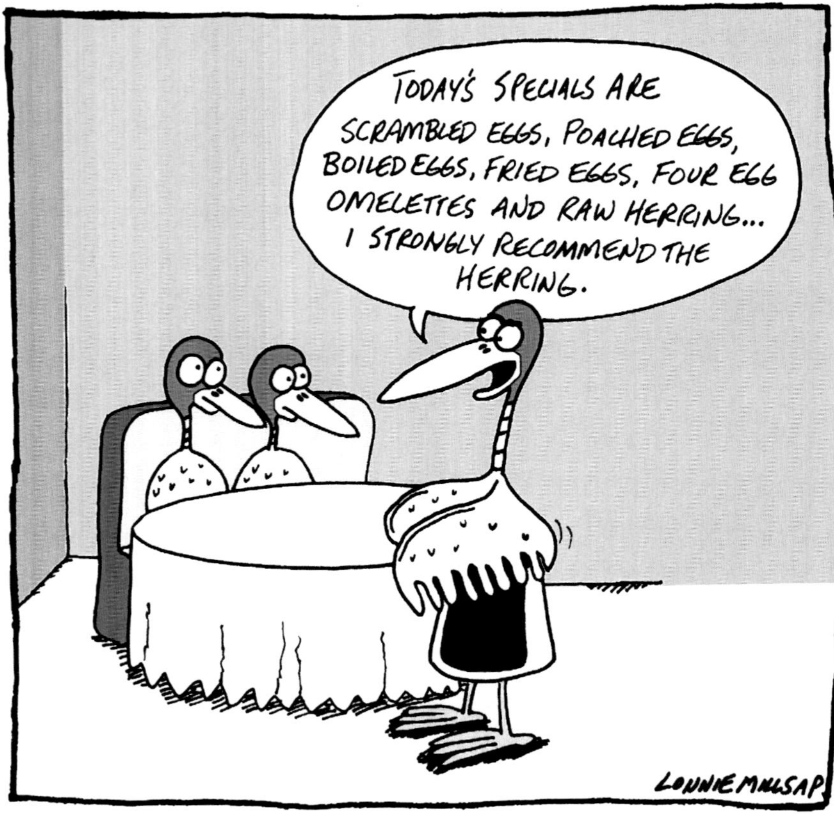
TODAY'S SPECIALS ARE SCRAMBLED EGGS, POACHED EGGS, BOILED EGGS, FRIED EGGS, FOUR EGG OMELETTES AND RAW HERRING... I STRONGLY RECOMMEND THE HERRING.
LONNIE MILLSAP

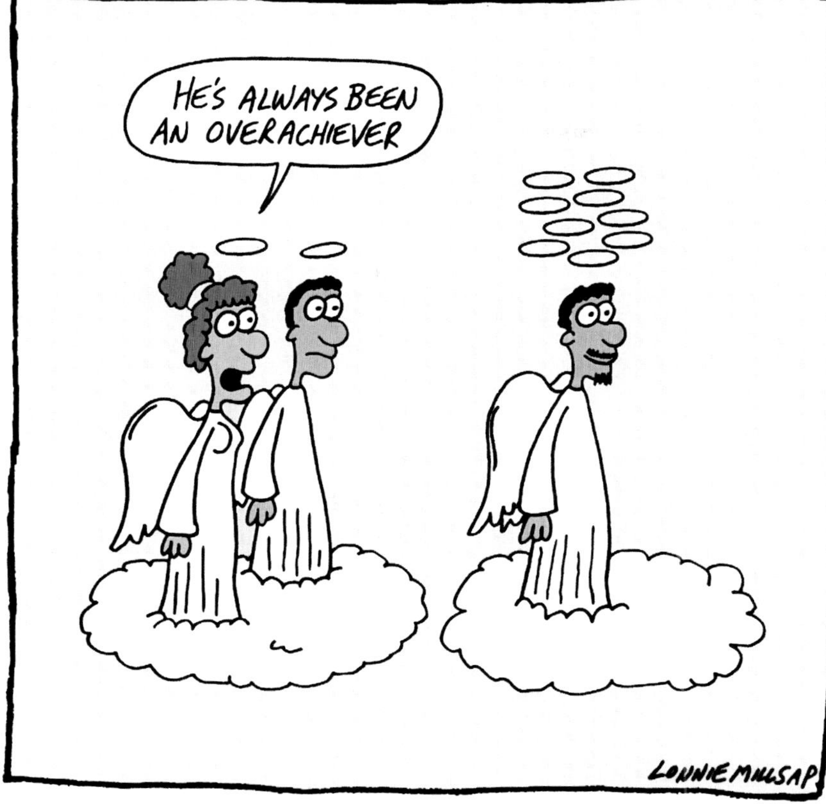
HE'S ALWAYS BEEN AN OVERACHIEVER
LONNIE MILLSAP

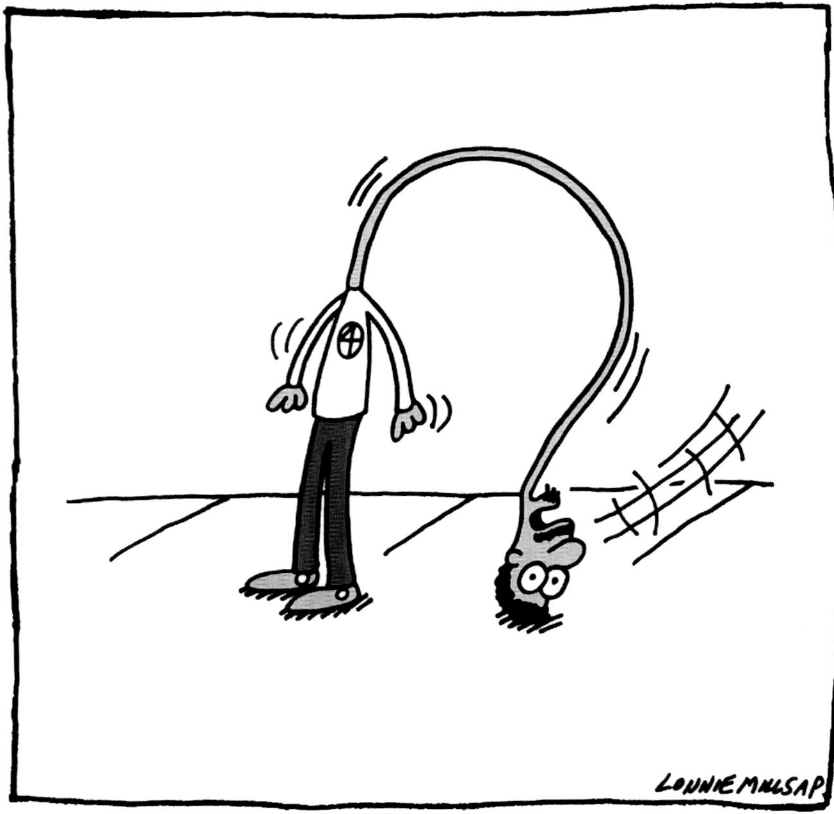
LONNIE MILLSAP

THE DANGER OF SNEEZING IF YOU ARE 'STRETCH' FROM THE FANTASTIC FOUR

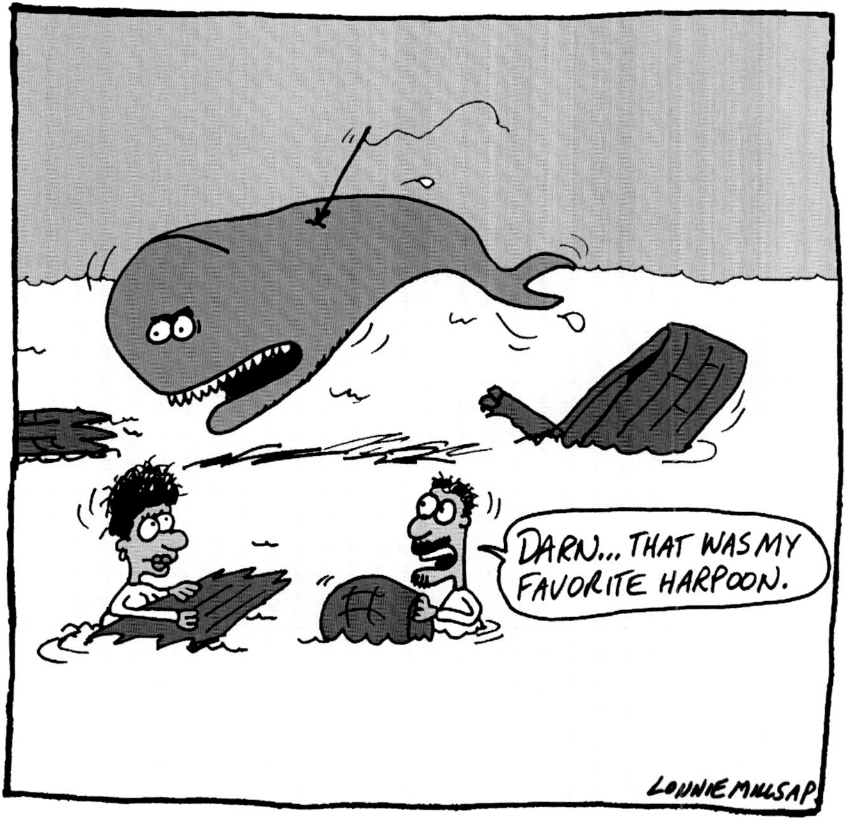
DARN... THAT WAS MY FAVORITE HARPOON.
LONNIE MILLSAP

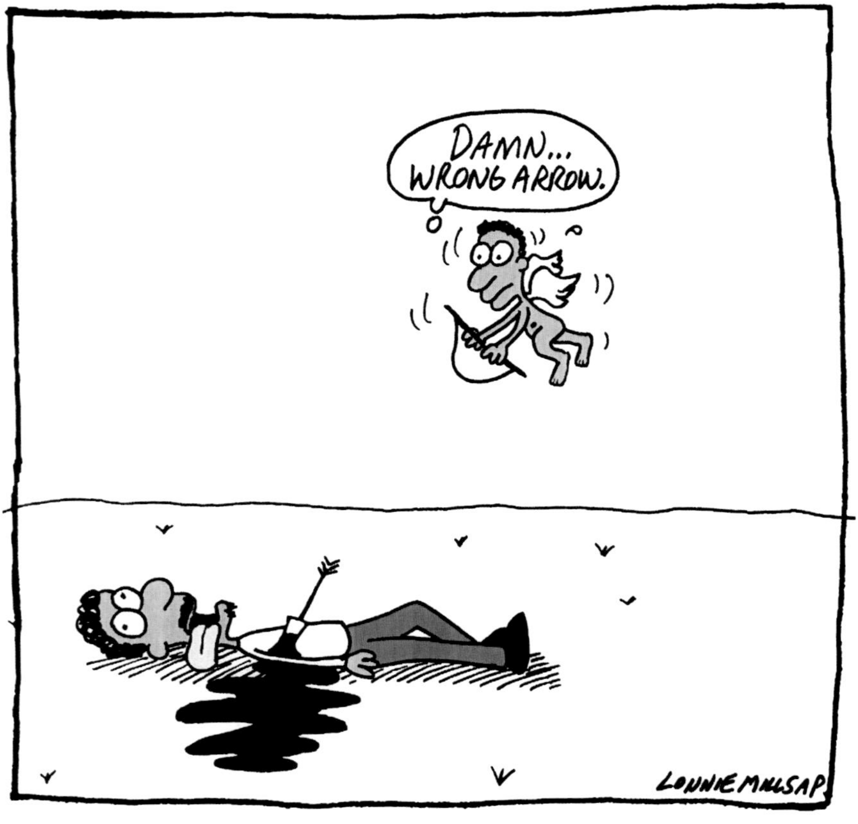
DAMN...
WRONG ARROW.
LONNIE MILLSAP

ONE OF CUPIDS RARE MISTAKES

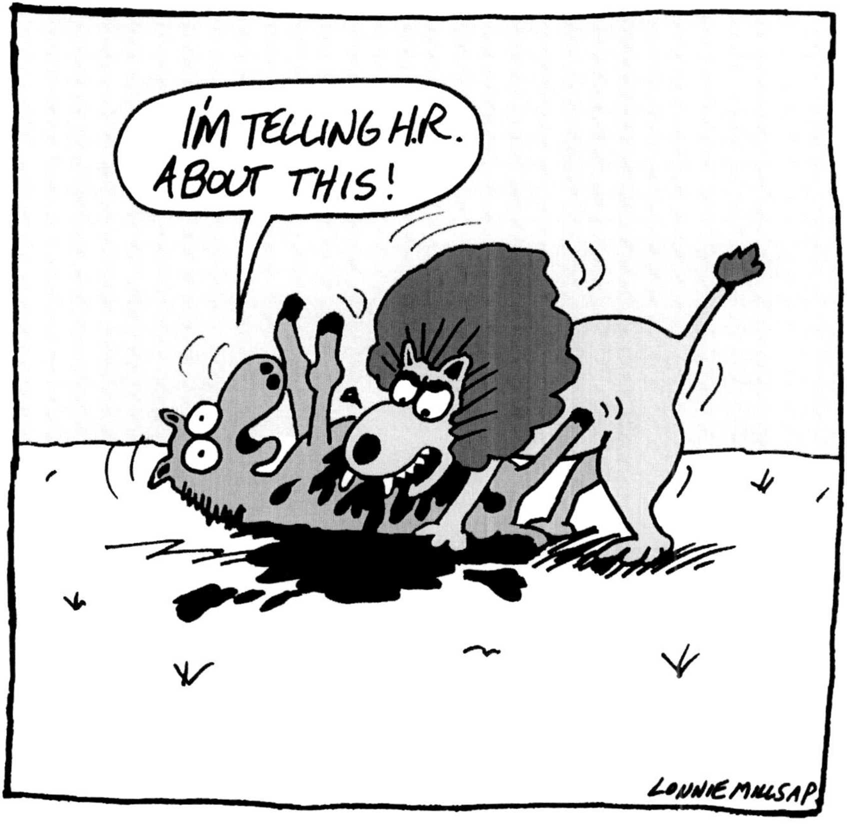
I'M TELLING H.R. ABOUT THIS!
LONNIE MILLSAP

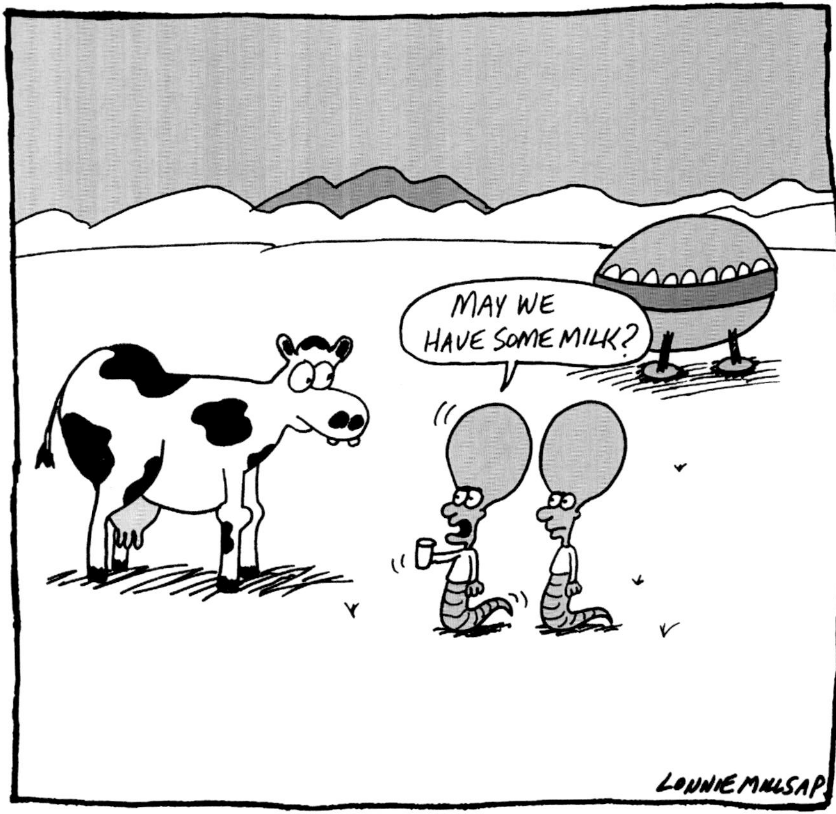
MAY WE HAVE SOME MILK?
LONNIE MILLSAP

WHY UFO'S LAND IN ISOLATED AREAS

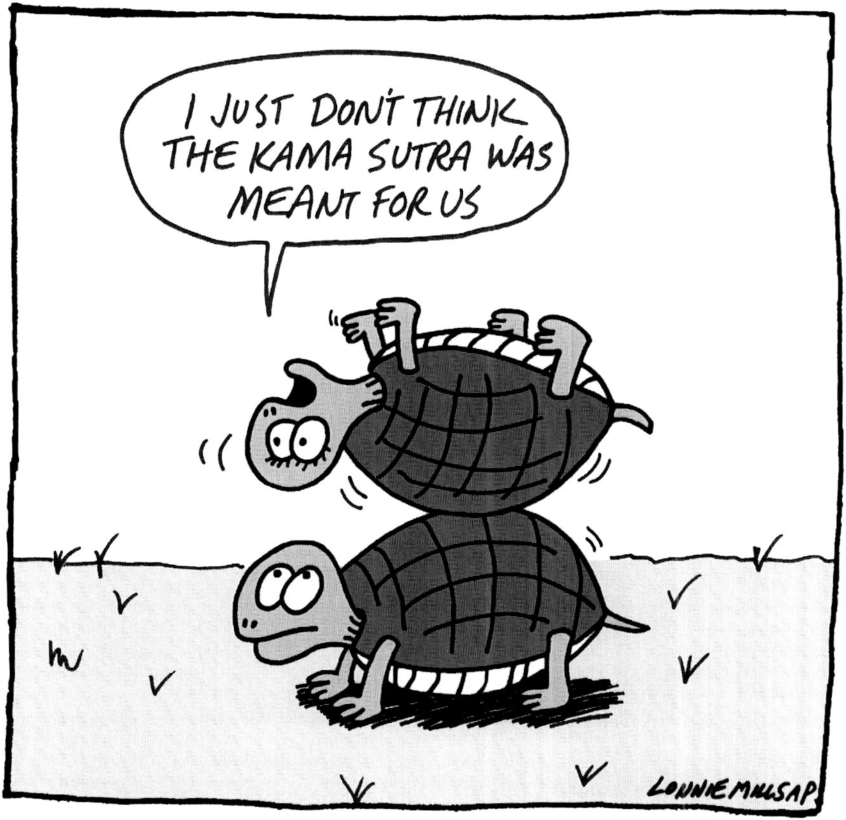
I JUST DON'T THINK THE KAMA SUTRA WAS MEANT FOR US
LONNIE MILLSAP

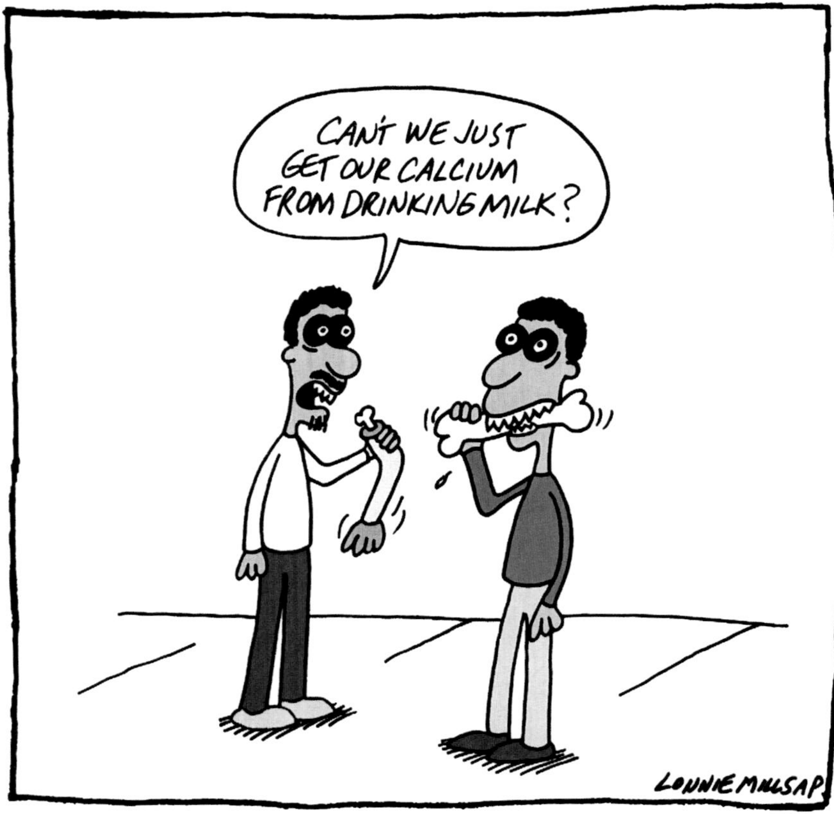
CAN'T WE JUST GET OUR CALCIUM FROM DRINKING MILK?
LONNIE MILLSAP

ZOMBIE TALK

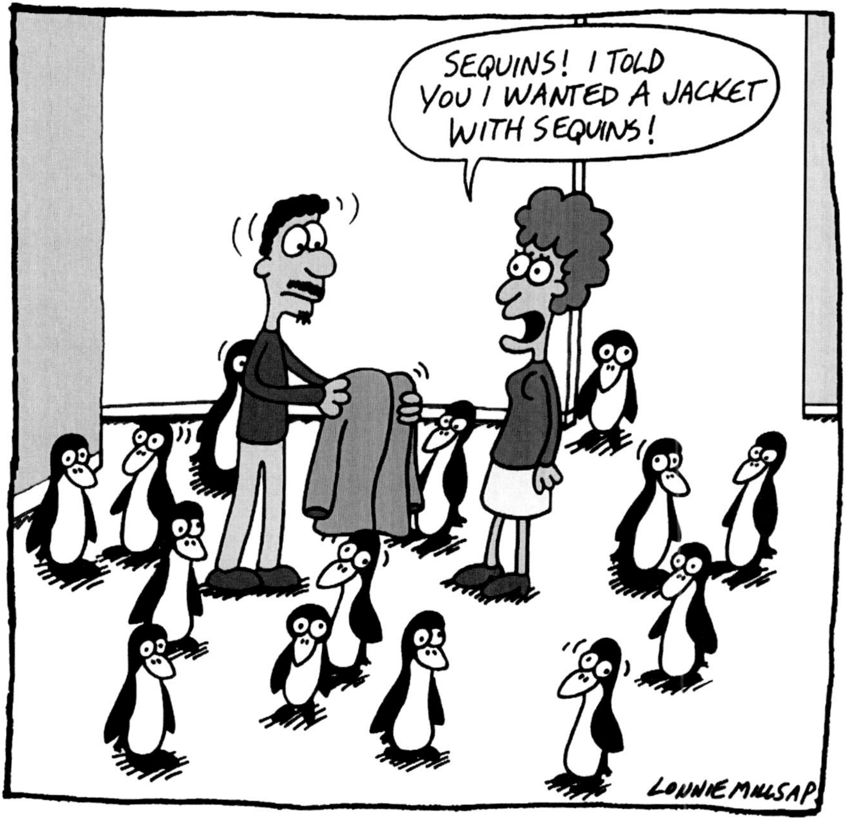
SEQUINS! I TOLD YOU I WANTED A JACKET WITH SEQUINS!
LONNIE MILLSAP

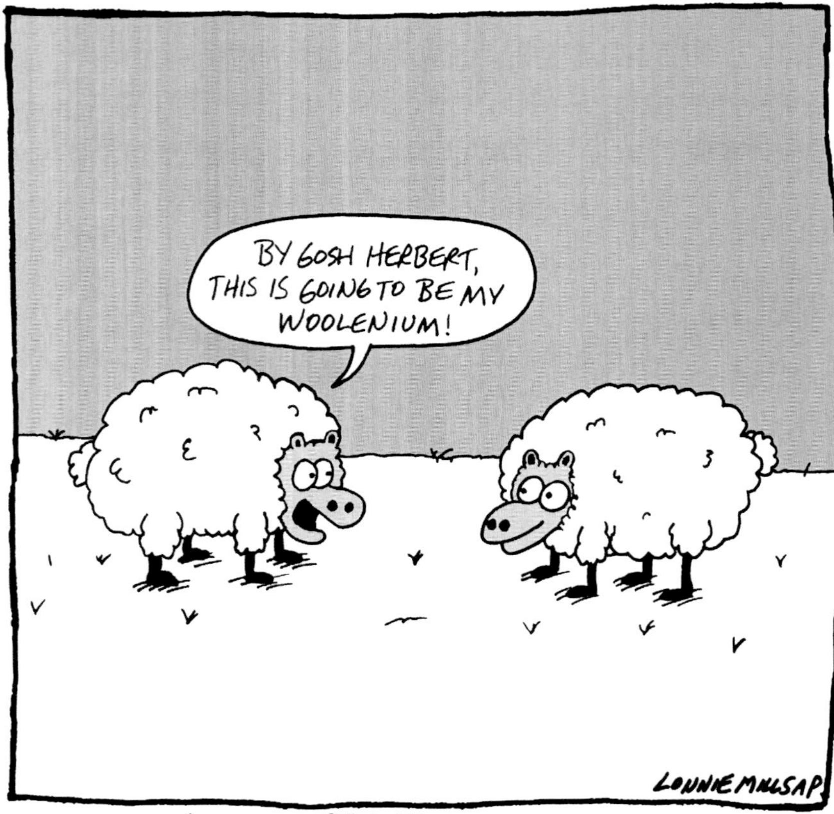
BY GOSH HERBERT, THIS IS GOING TO BE MY WOOLENIUM!
LONNIE MILLSAP

A SHEEP OPTIMIST IN THE YEAR 2000

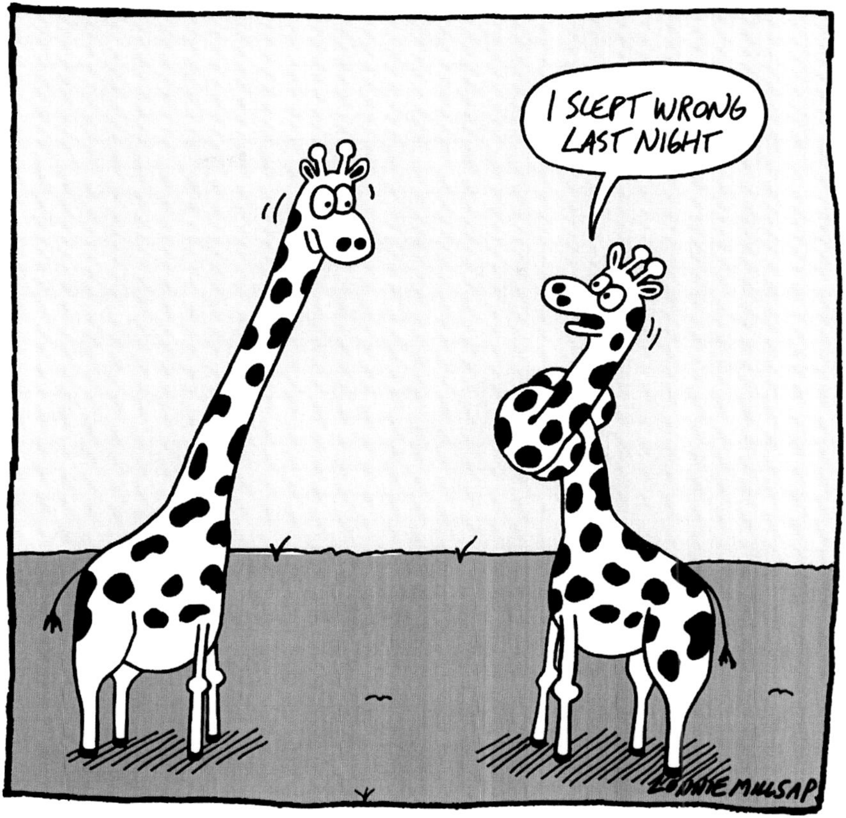
I SLEPT WRONG LAST NIGHT
RONNIE MILLSAP

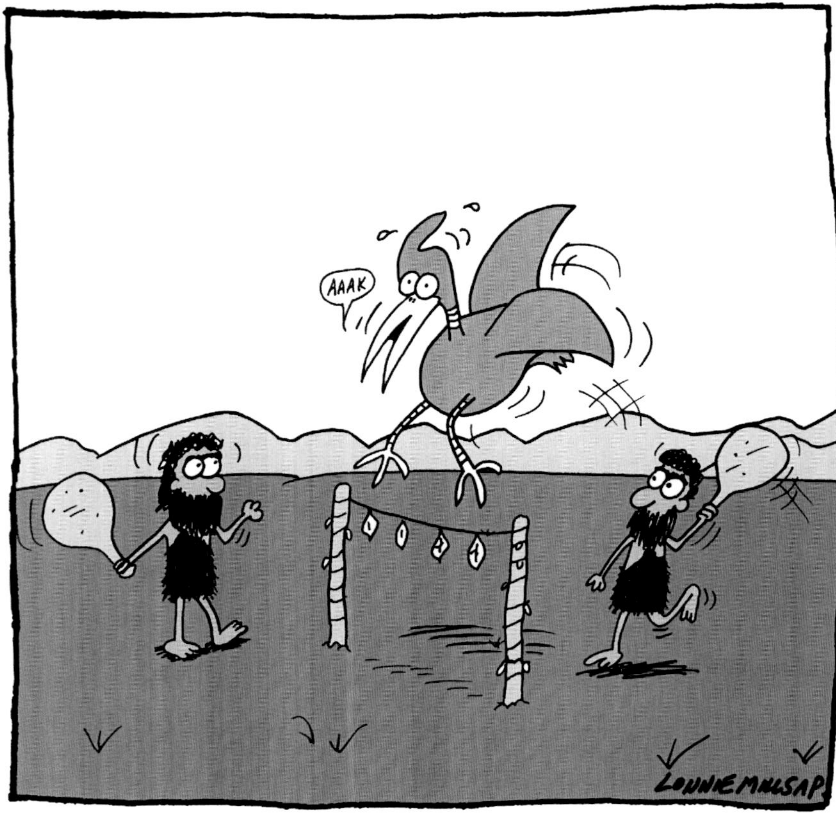
AAAK
LONNIE MILLSAP

PRE-HISTORIC BADMINTON

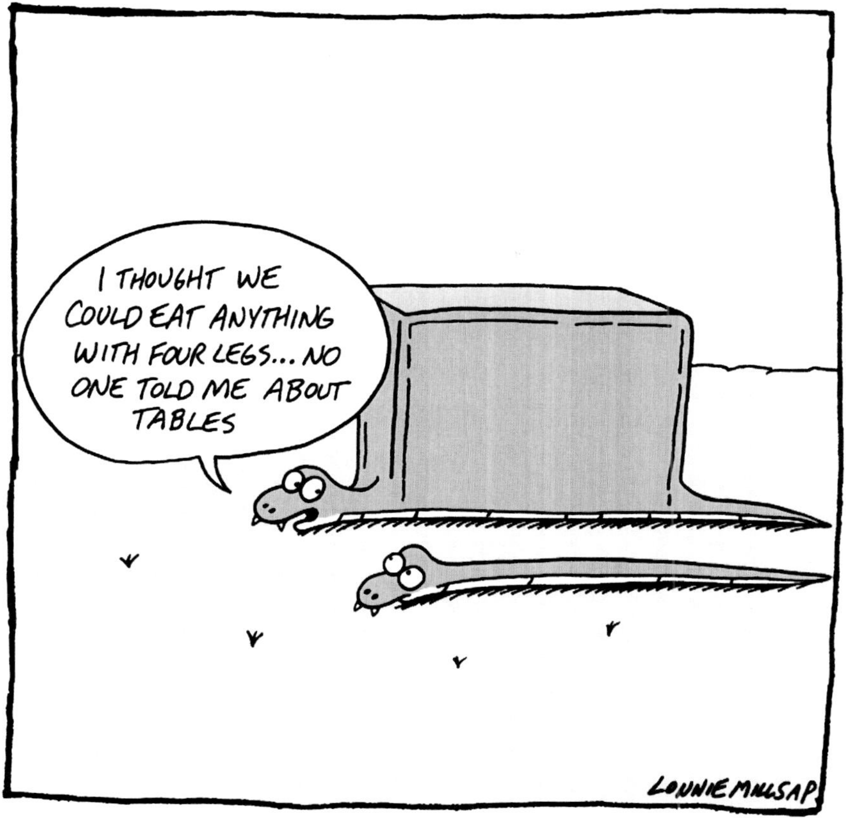
I THOUGHT WE COULD EAT ANYTHING WITH FOUR LEGS... NO ONE TOLD ME ABOUT TABLES
LONNIE MILLSAP

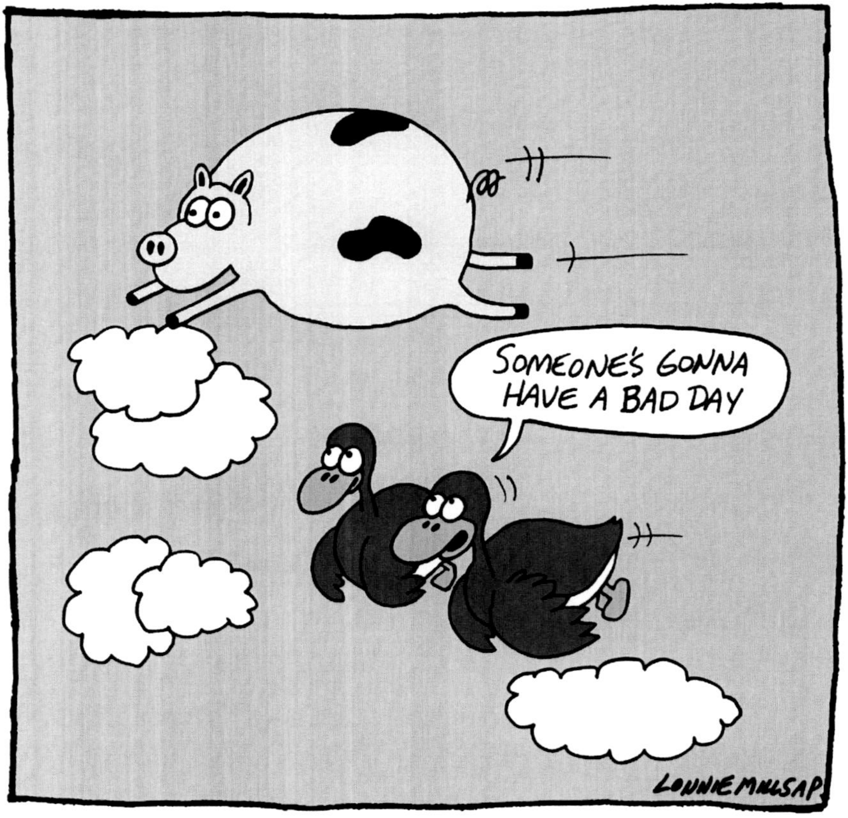
SOMEONE'S GONNA HAVE A BAD DAY
LONNIE MILLSAP

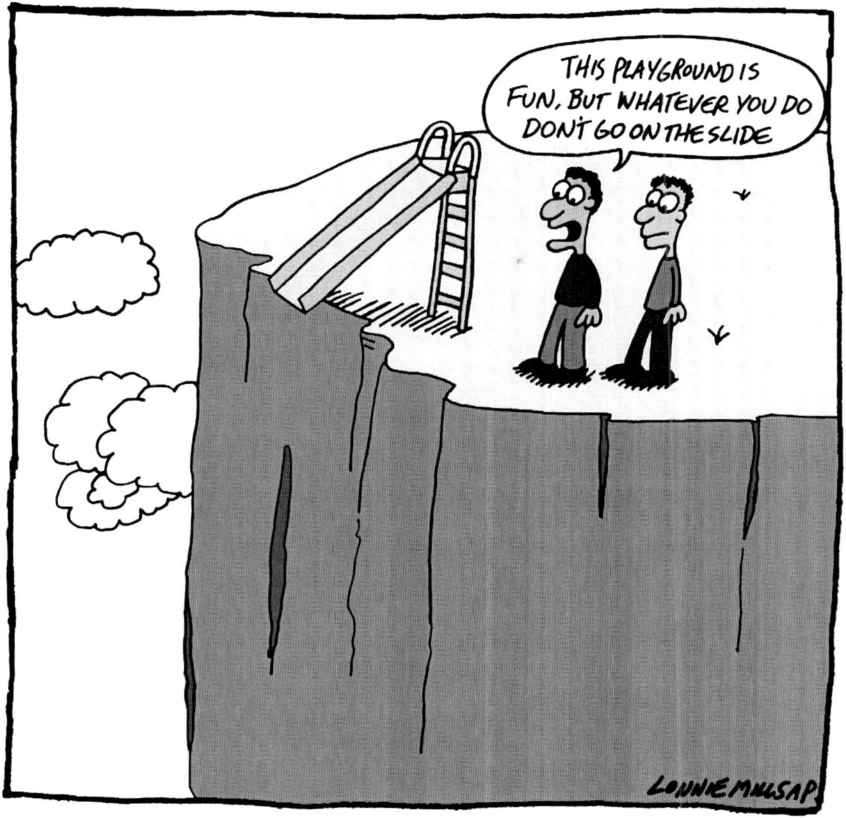
THIS PLAYGROUND IS FUN, BUT WHATEVER YOU DO DON'T GO ON THE SLIDE
LONNIE MILLSAP

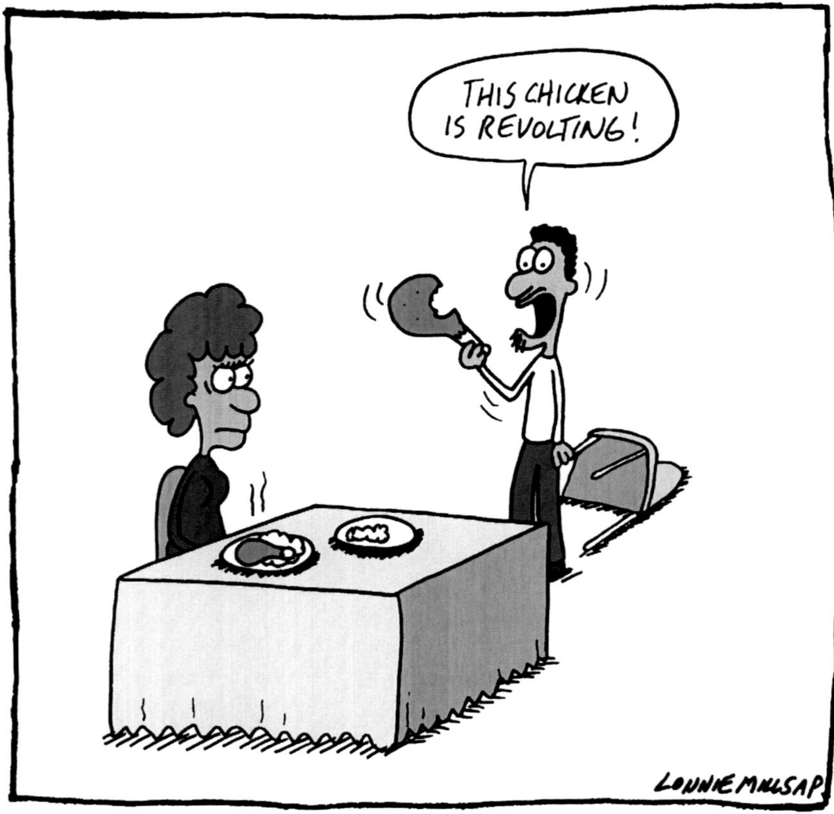
THIS CHICKEN IS REVOLTING!
LONNIE MILLSAP

WHEN CHICKEN REVOLTS POSTHUMOUSLY

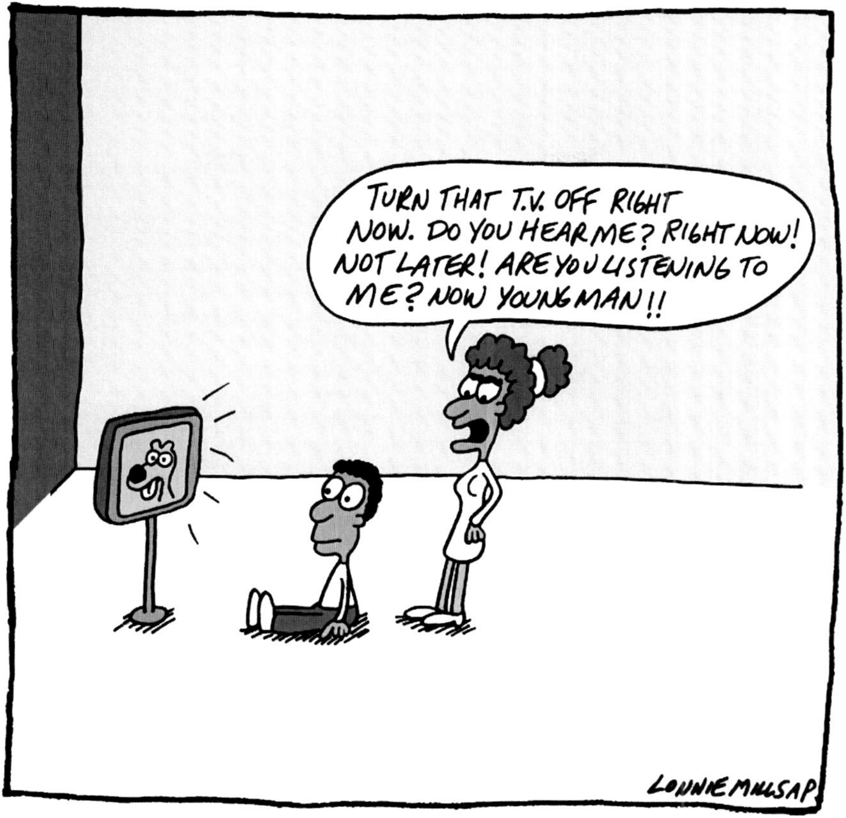
TURN THAT T.V. OFF RIGHT NOW. DO YOU HEAR ME? RIGHT NOW! NOT LATER! ARE YOU LISTENING TO ME? NOW YOUNG MAN!!
LONNIE MILLSAP

WHEN PARENTS DON'T SAY 'SIMON SAYS'

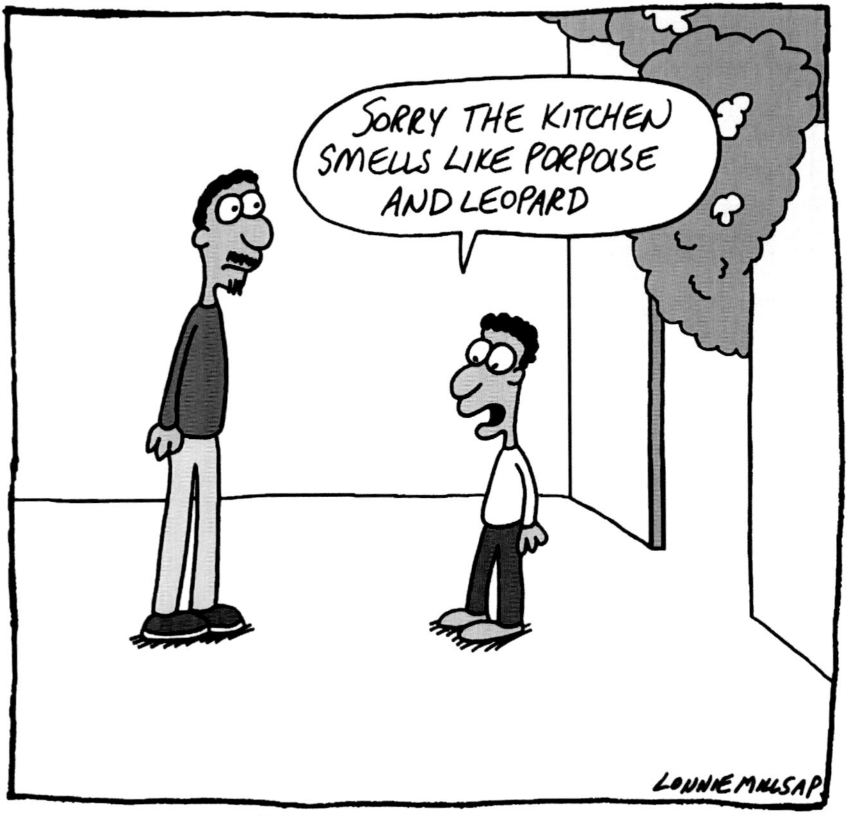
SORRY THE KITCHEN SMELLS LIKE PORPOISE AND LEOPARD
LONNIE MILLSAP

A SINCERE YET DISTURBING APOLOGY

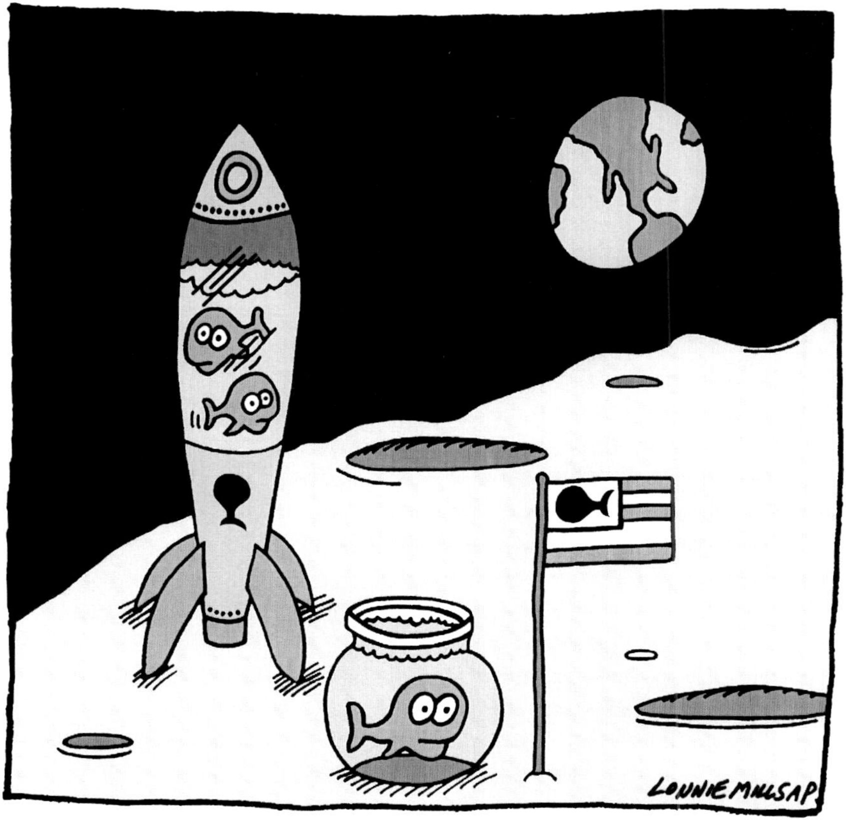
LONNIE MILLSAP

TWO BILLION YEARS BEFORE MAN:
WHEN FISH RULED THE WORLD

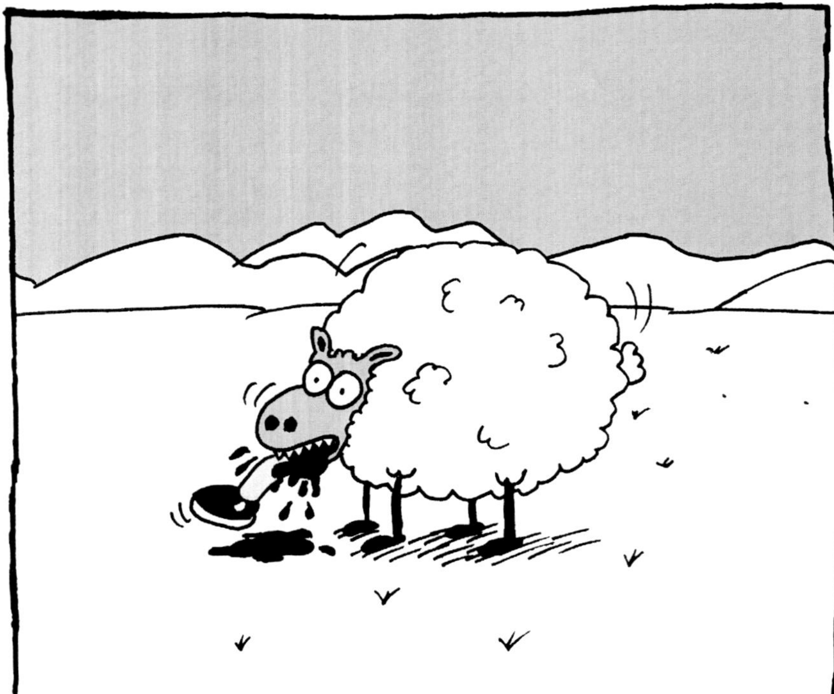
LONNIE MILLSAP

THE SIDE EFFECTS OF GLOBAL WARMING CAN RESULT IN UNUSUAL BEHAVIOR IN SOME ANIMALS

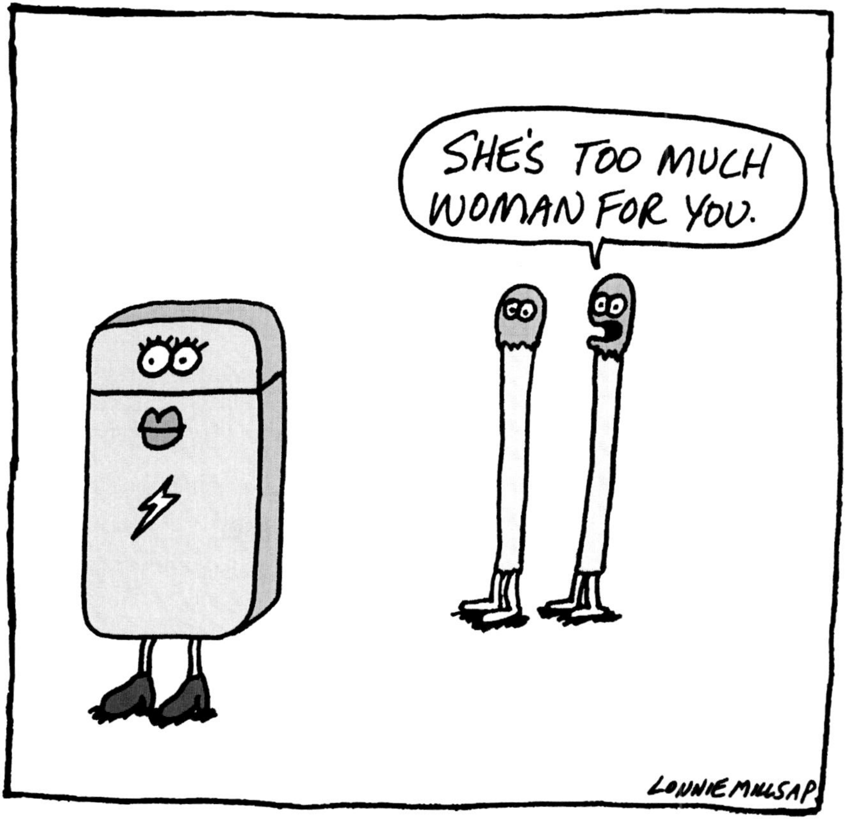
SHE'S TOO MUCH WOMAN FOR YOU.
LONNIE MILLSAP

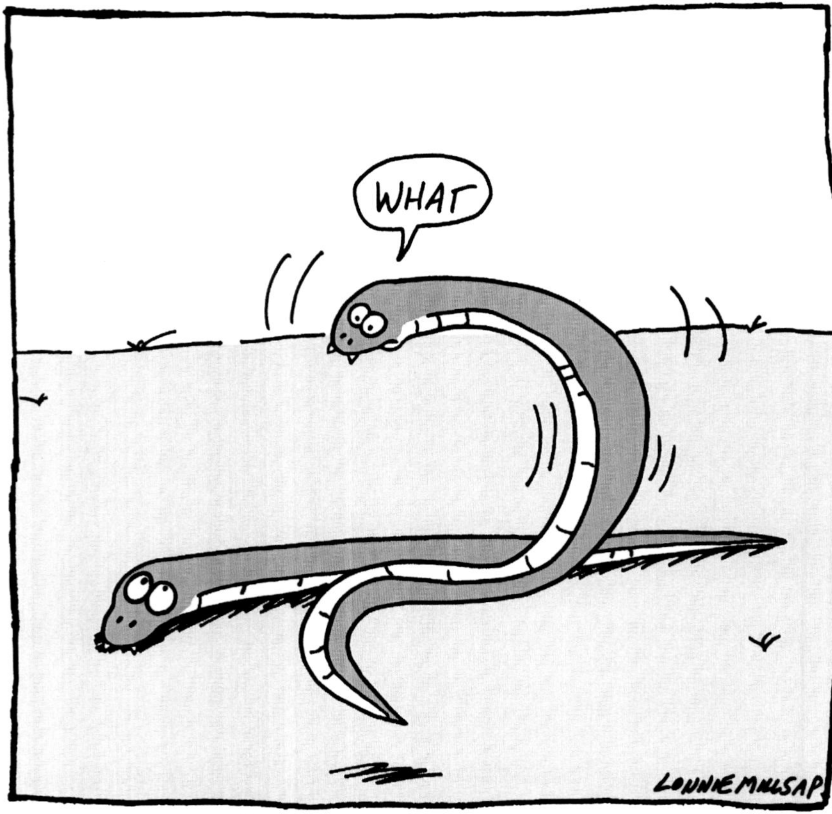
WHAT
LONNIE MILLSAP

SNAKE PUNCTUATION

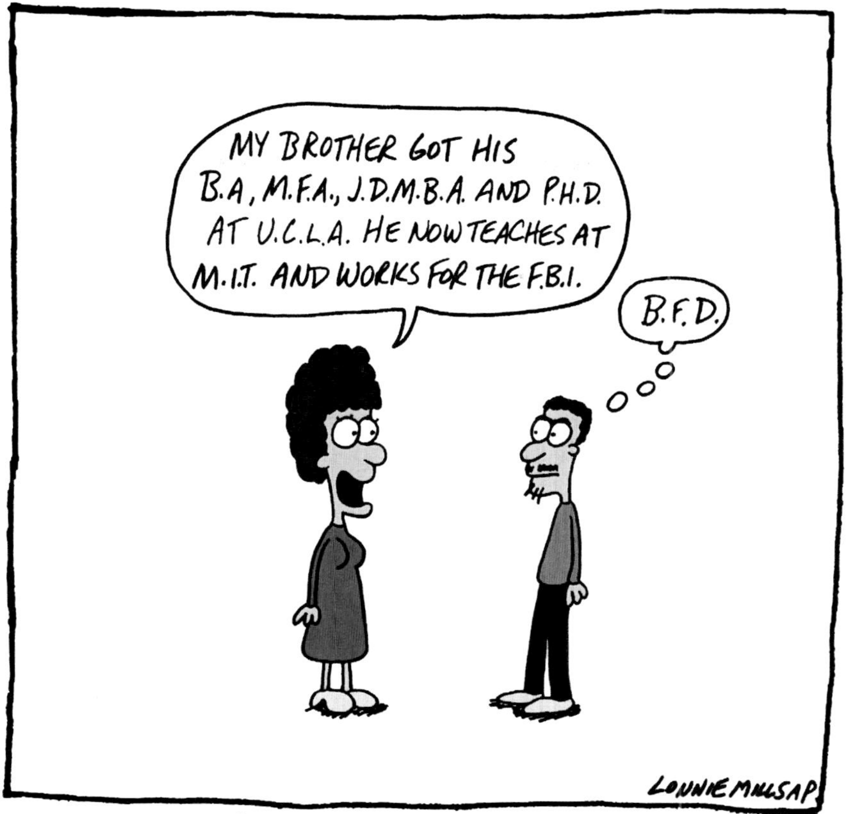
MY BROTHER GOT HIS B.A, M.F.A., J.D.M.B.A. AND P.H.D. AT U.C.L.A. HE NOW TEACHES AT M.I.T. AND WORKS FOR THE F.B.I.
B.F.D.
LONNIE MILLSAP

BOB KNOWS HOW TO ABBREVIATE TOO

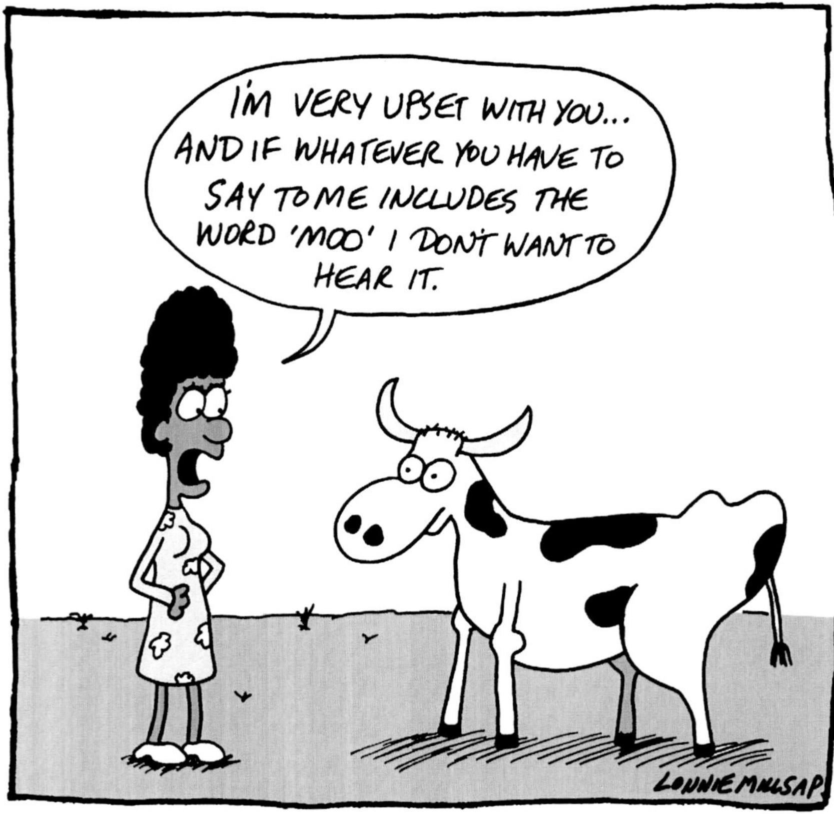
I'M VERY UPSET WITH YOU... AND IF WHATEVER YOU HAVE TO SAY TO ME INCLUDES THE WORD 'MOO' I DON'T WANT TO HEAR IT.
LONNIE MILLSAP

INTERSPECIES DISAGREEMENTS

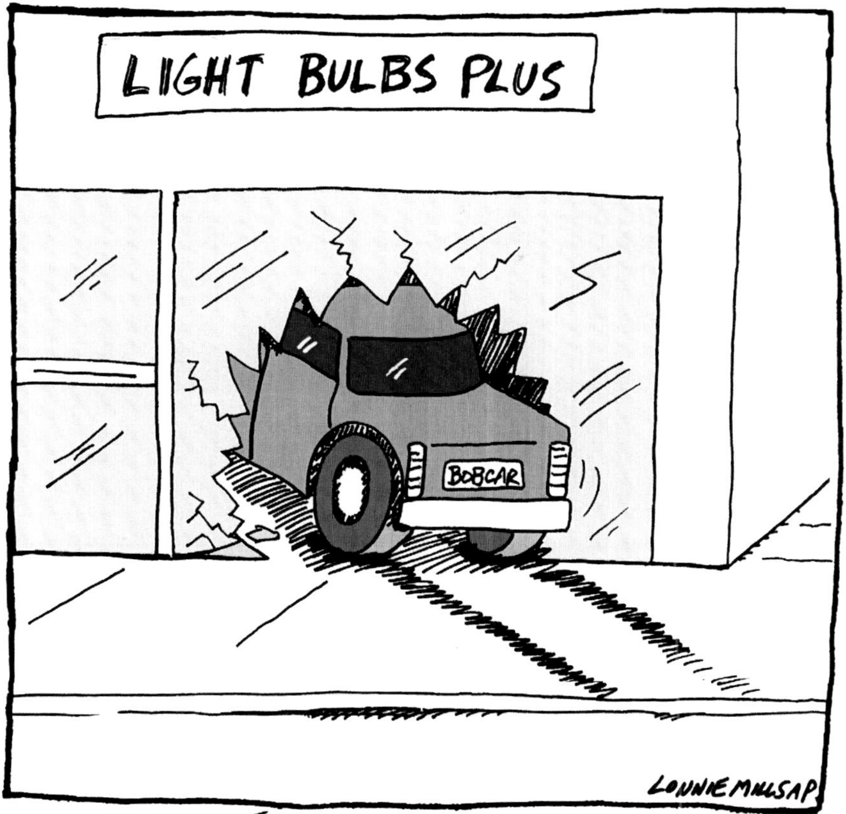
LIGHT BULBS PLUS
BOBCAR
LONNIE MILLSAP

THERE MUST BE A MOTH
SOMEWHERE IN BOB'S FAMILY TREE

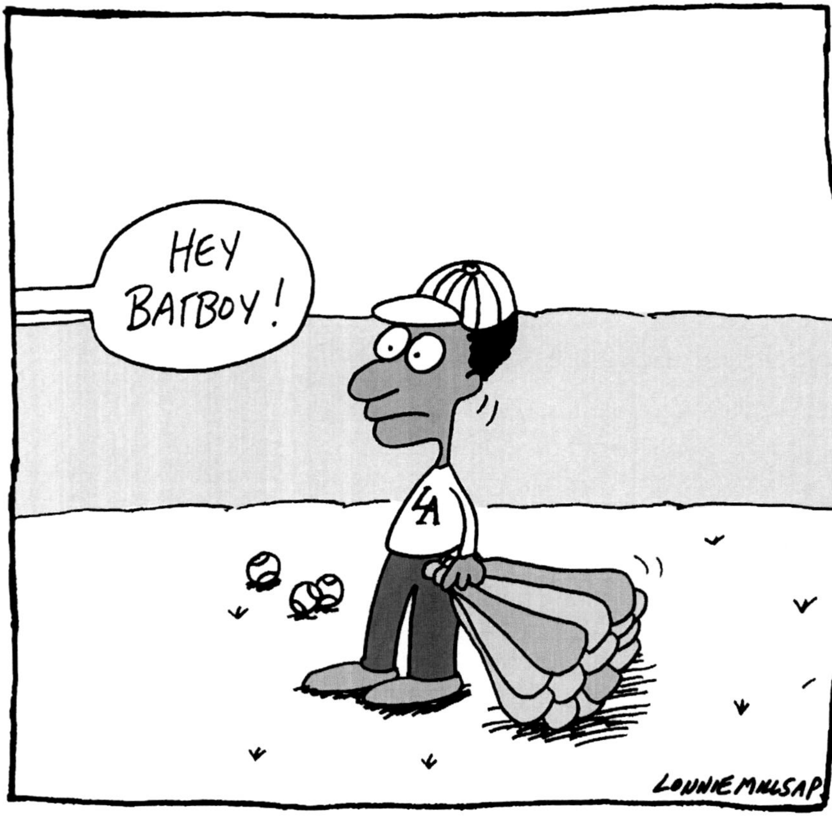
HEY BATBOY!
LONNIE MILLSAP

BATMAN AS A KID

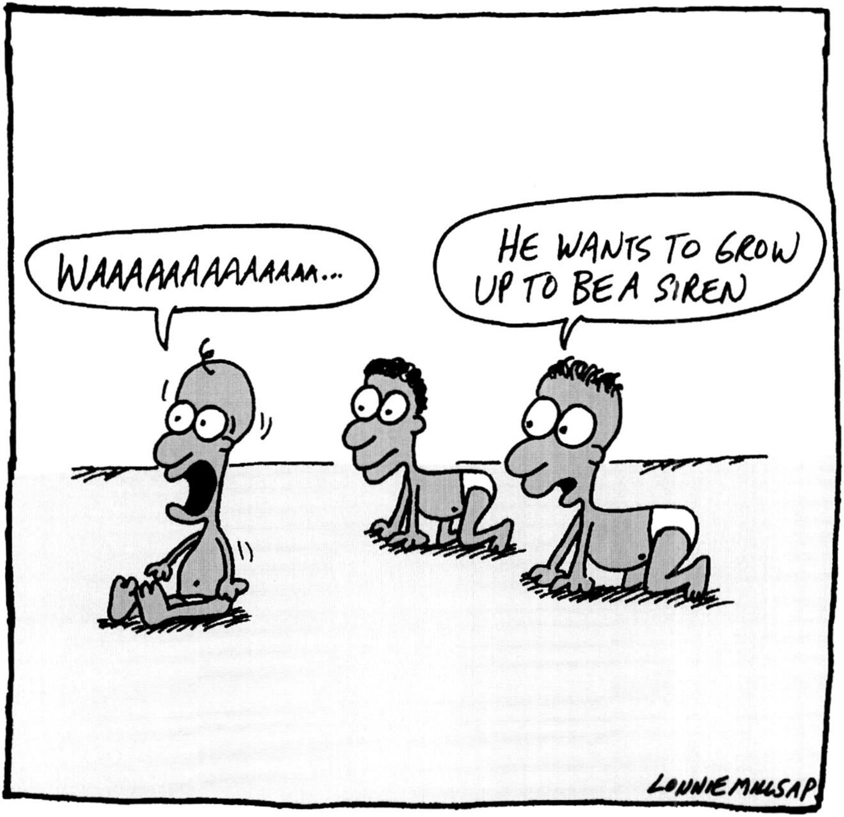
WAAAAAAAAAAAAA...
HE WANTS TO GROW UP TO BE A SIREN
LONNIE MILLSAP

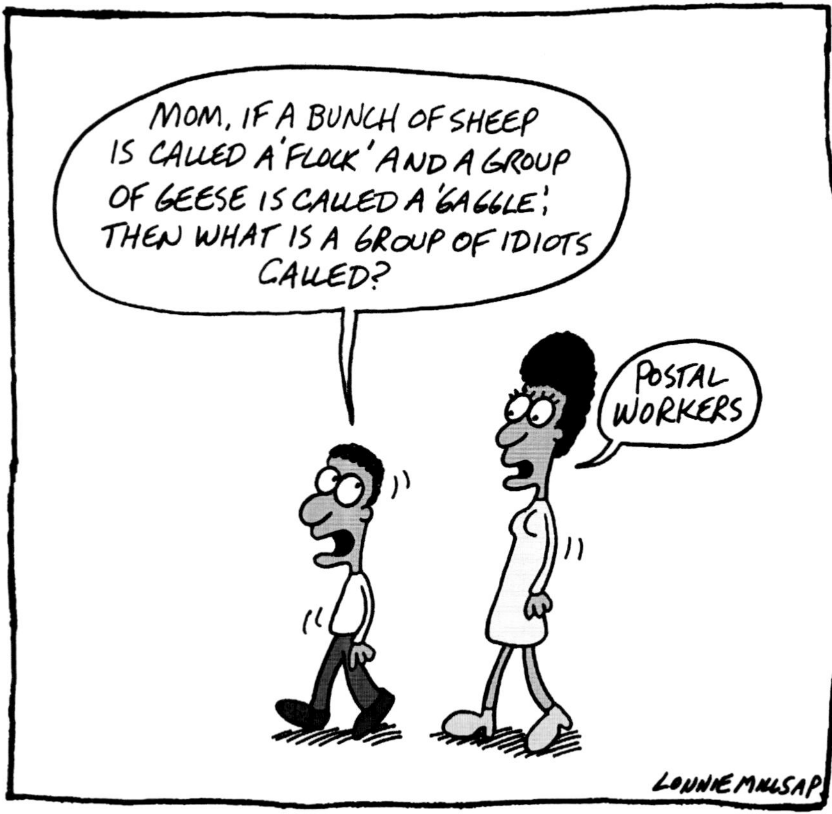
MOM, IF A BUNCH OF SHEEP IS CALLED A 'FLOCK' AND A GROUP OF GEESE IS CALLED A 'GAGGLE', THEN WHAT IS A GROUP OF IDIOTS CALLED?
POSTAL WORKERS
LONNIE MILLSAP

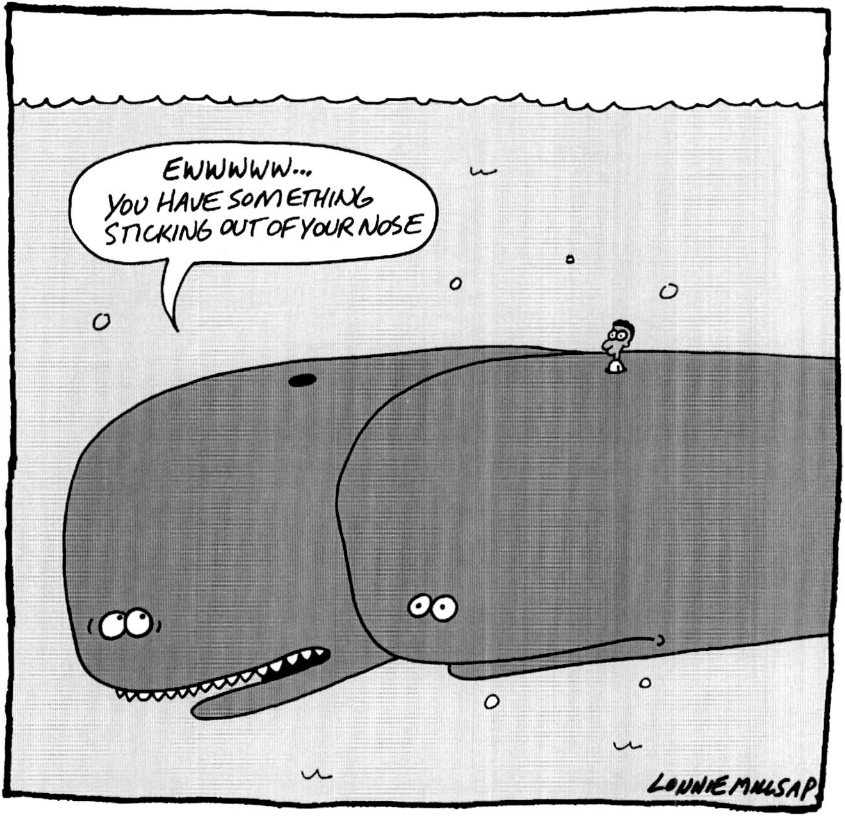
EWWWWW... YOU HAVE SOMETHING STICKING OUT OF YOUR NOSE
LONNIE MILLSAP

A COMPELLING REASON FOR CREATING WHALE KLEENEX

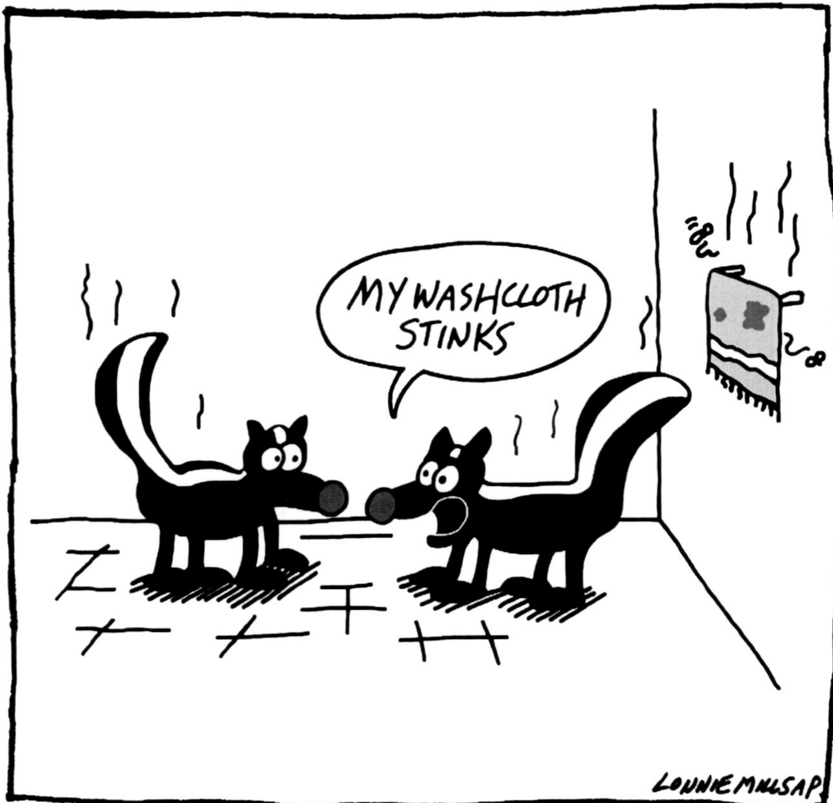
MY WASHCLOTH STINKS
LONNIE MILLSAP

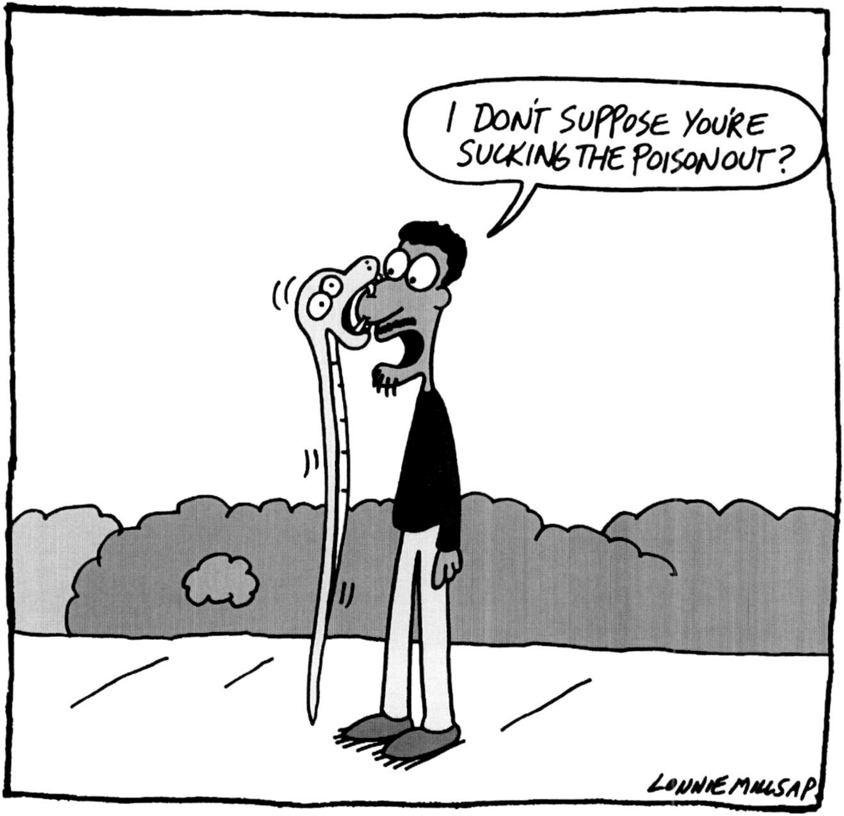
I DON'T SUPPOSE YOU'RE SUCKING THE POISON OUT?
LONNIE MILLSAP

BOB IS SUCH AN OPTIMIST

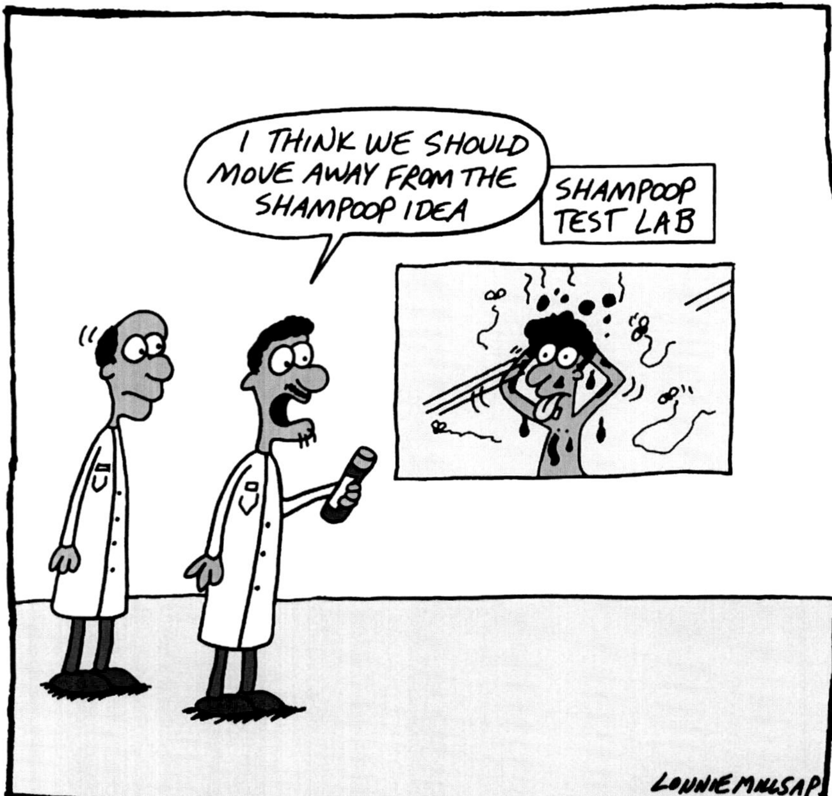
I THINK WE SHOULD MOVE AWAY FROM THE SHAMPOOP IDEA
SHAMPOOP TEST LAB
LONNIE MILLSAP

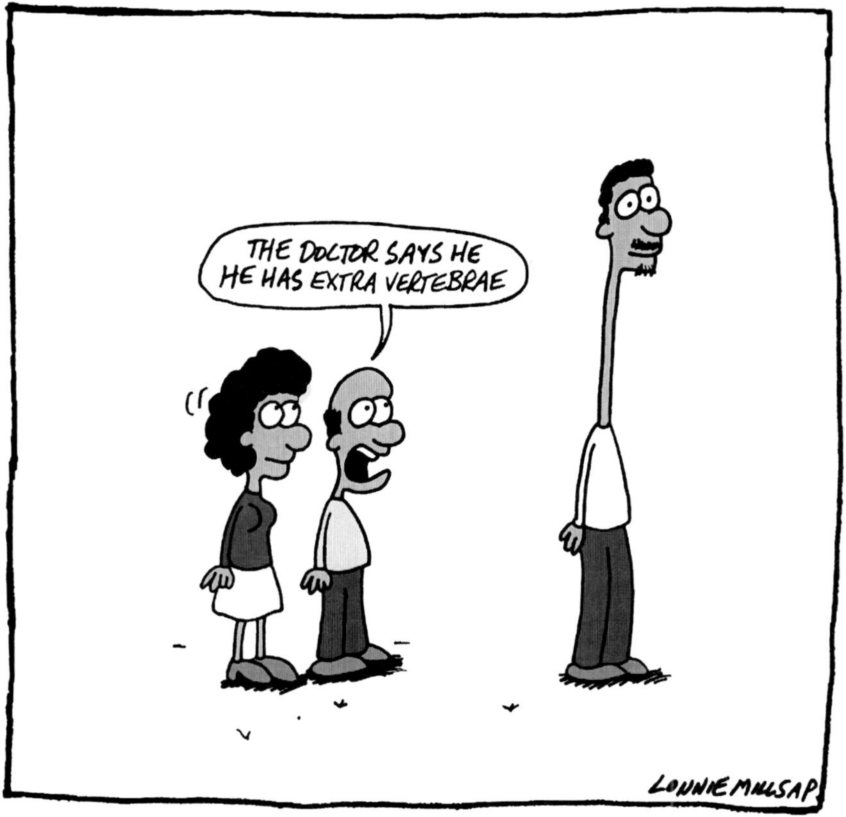
THE DOCTOR SAYS HE
HE HAS EXTRA VERTEBRAE
LONNIE MILLSAP

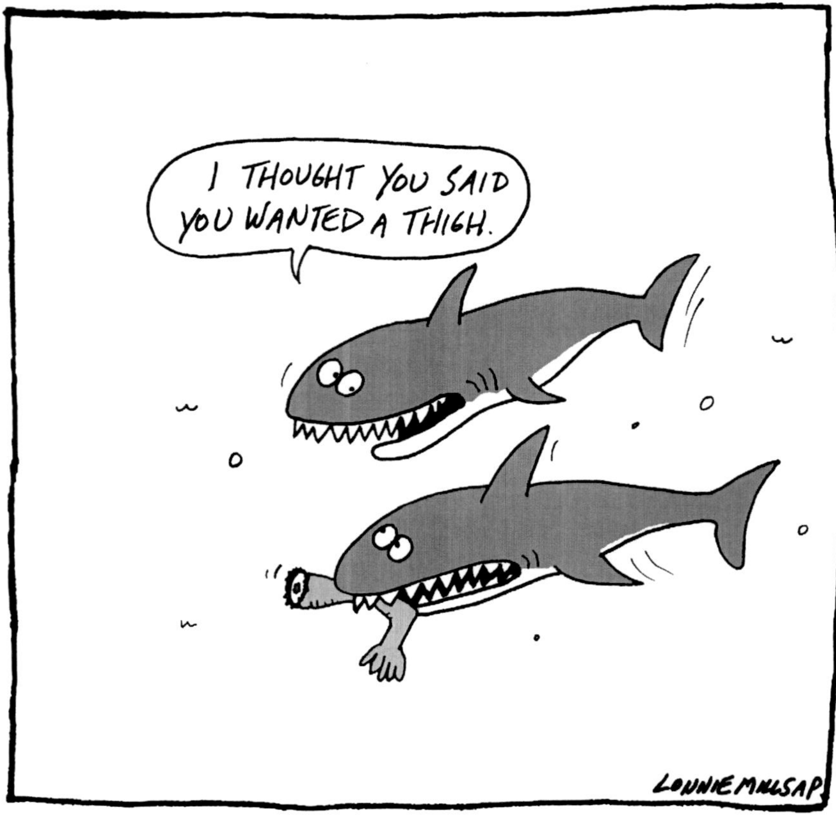
I THOUGHT YOU SAID YOU WANTED A THIGH.
LONNIE MILLSAP

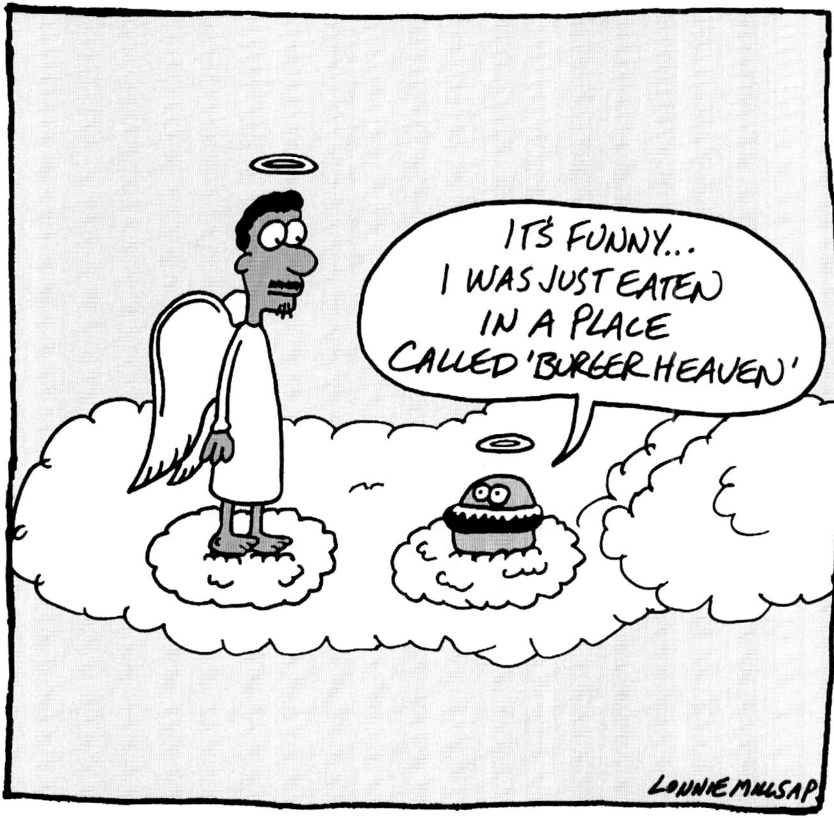
IT'S FUNNY...
I WAS JUST EATEN
IN A PLACE
CALLED 'BURGER HEAVEN'
LONNIE MILLSAP

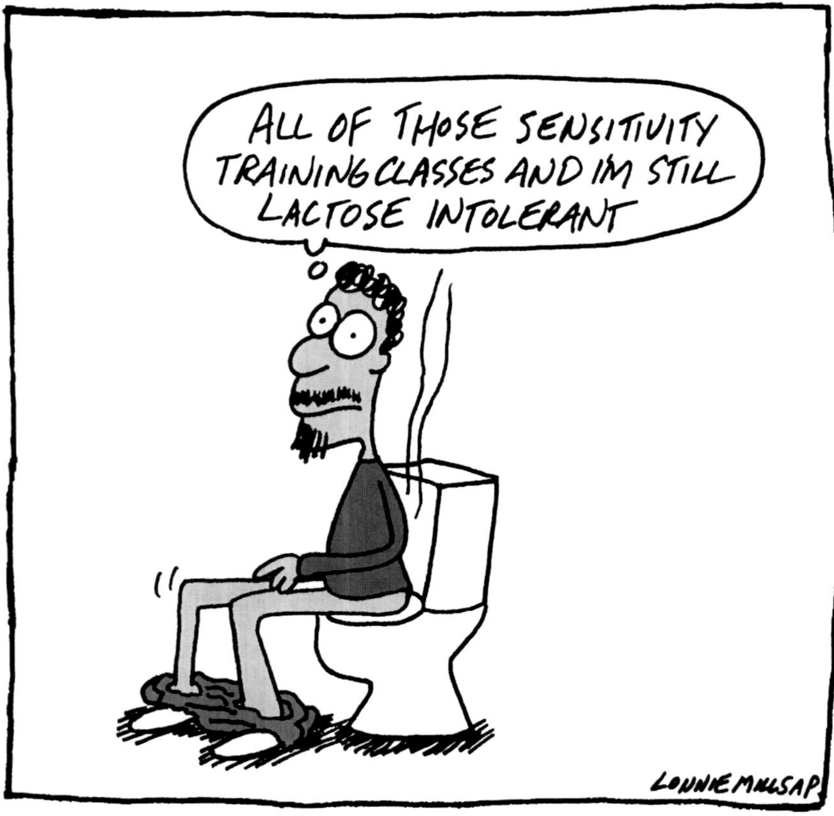
ALL OF THOSE SENSITIVITY TRAINING CLASSES AND IM STILL LACTOSE INTOLERANT
LONNIE MILLSAP

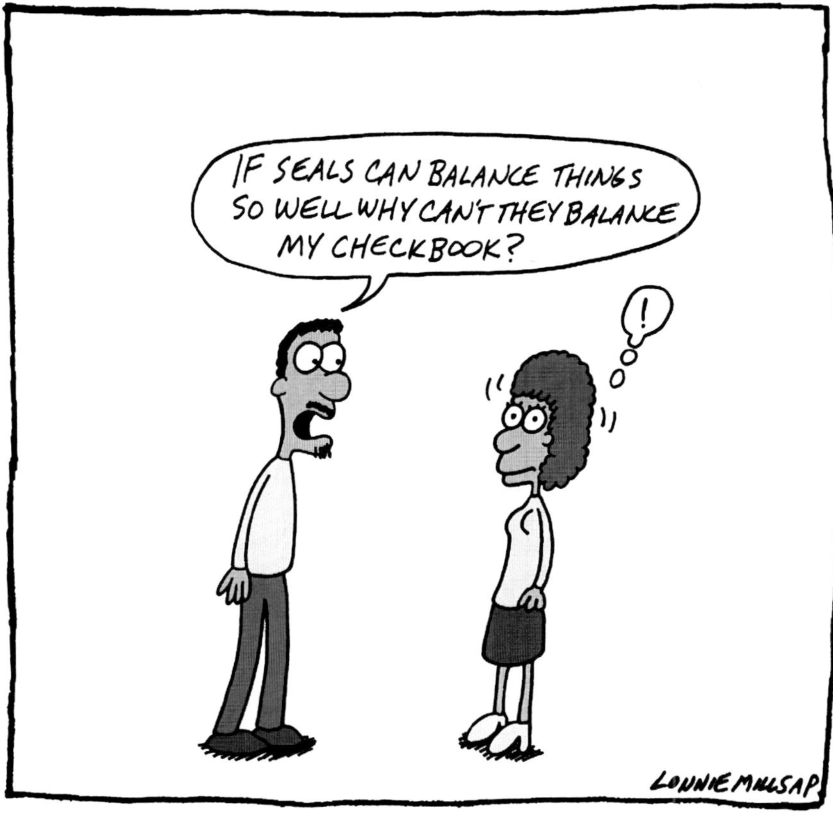
IF SEALS CAN BALANCE THINGS SO WELL WHY CAN'T THEY BALANCE MY CHECKBOOK?
!
LONNIE MILLSAP

IT BECAME CLEAR TO IRMA THAT SHE WOULD HANDLE THE FINANCES FROM THIS POINT ON

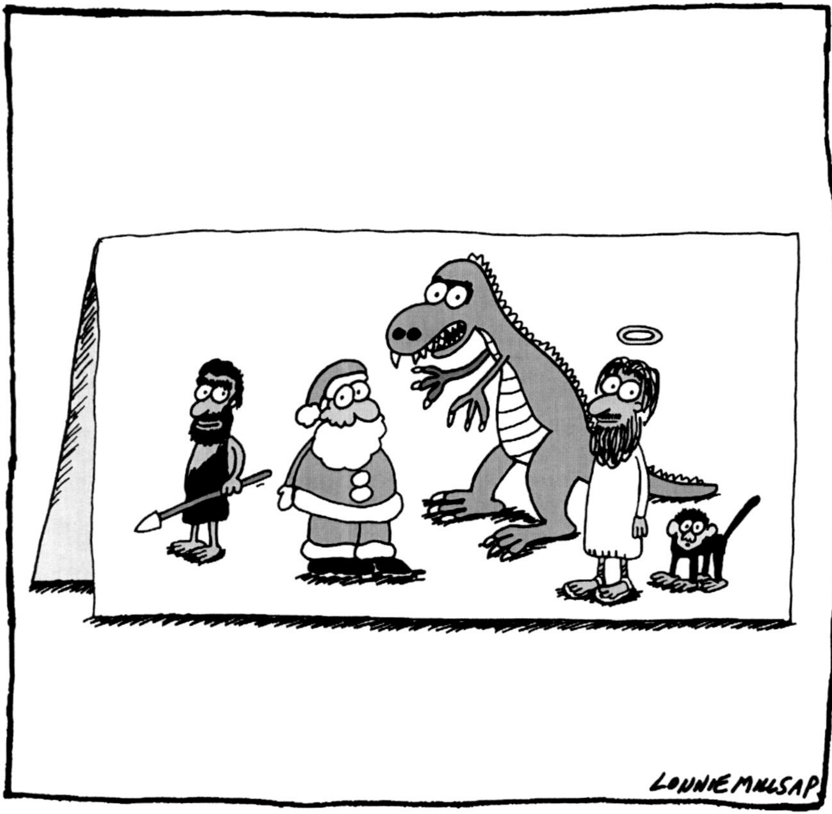
LONNIE MILLSAP

THE FIRST INTELLIGENT DESIGN GREETING CARD

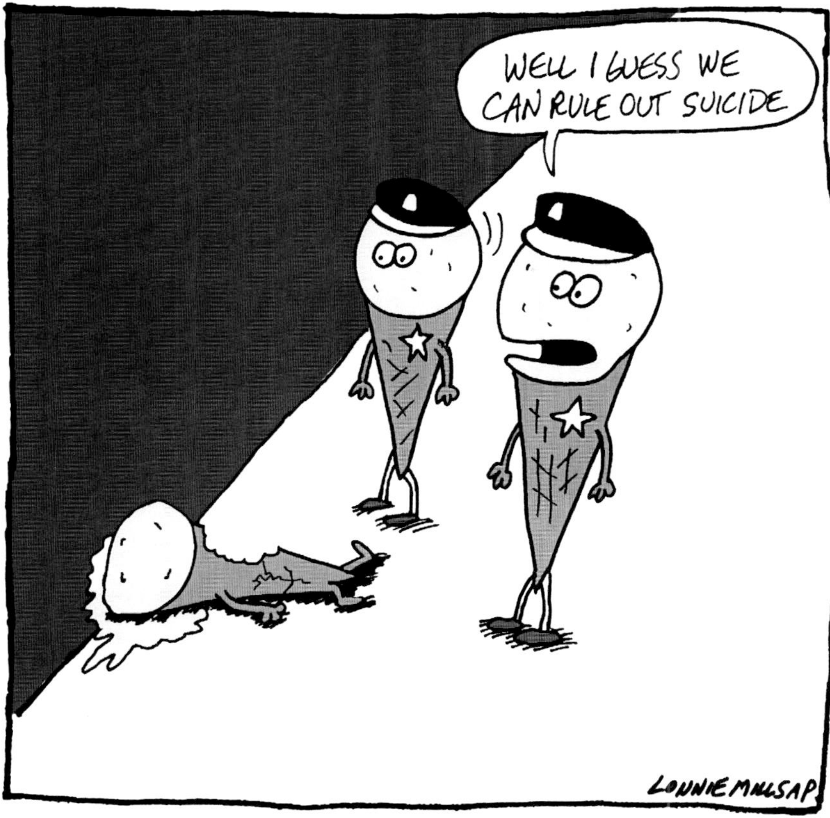
WELL I GUESS WE CAN RULE OUT SUICIDE
LONNIE MILLSAP

THE ICE CREAM POLICE

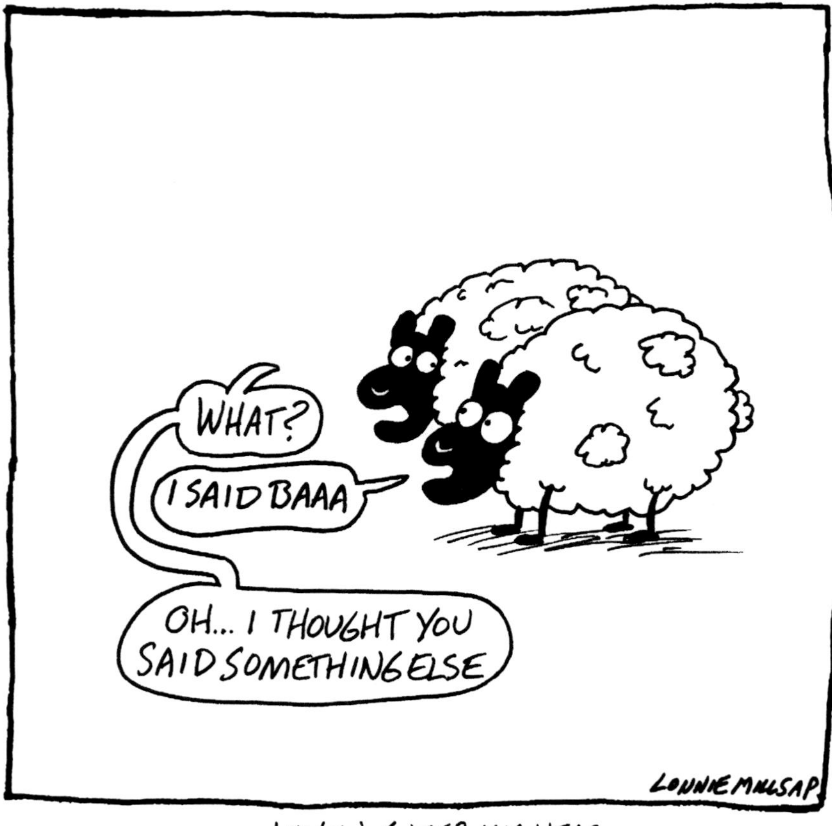
WHAT?
I SAID BAAA
OH... I THOUGHT YOU SAID SOMETHING ELSE
LONNIE MILLSAP

WHEN SHEEP MIS-HEAR

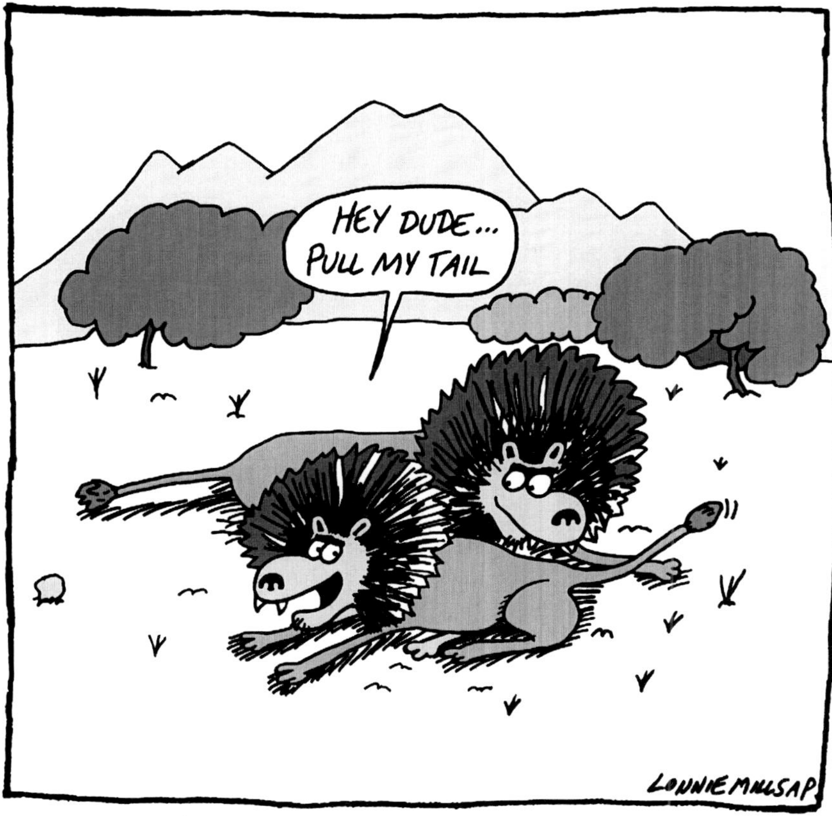
HEY DUDE...
PULL MY TAIL
LONNIE MILLSAP

JUVENILE BEHAVIOR... IN THE JUNGLE

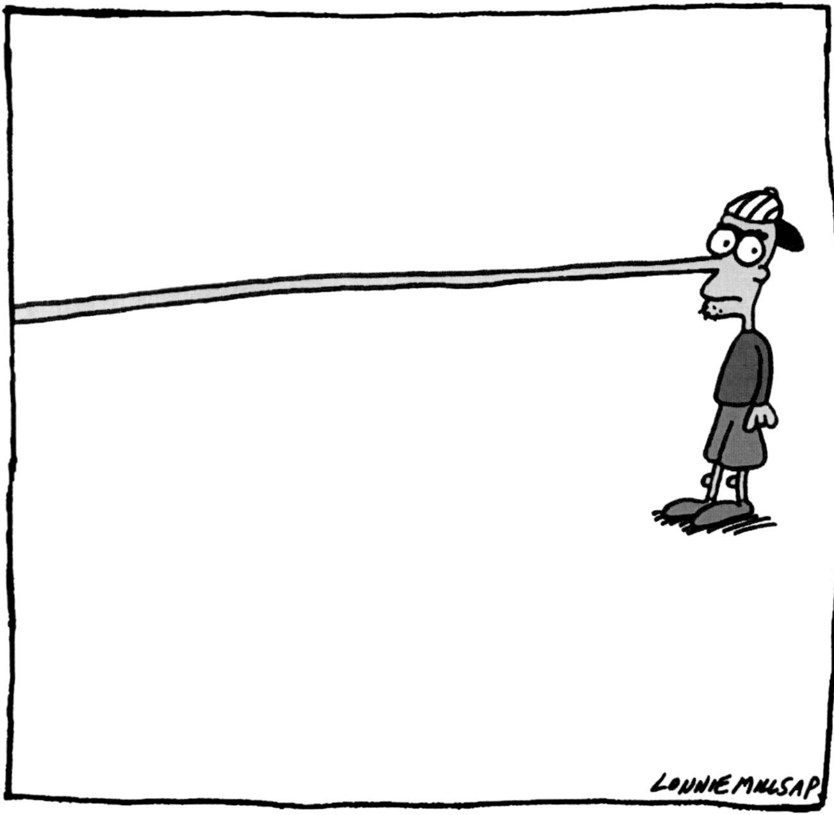
LONNIE MILLSAP

PINOCCHIO- THE TEENAGE YEARS

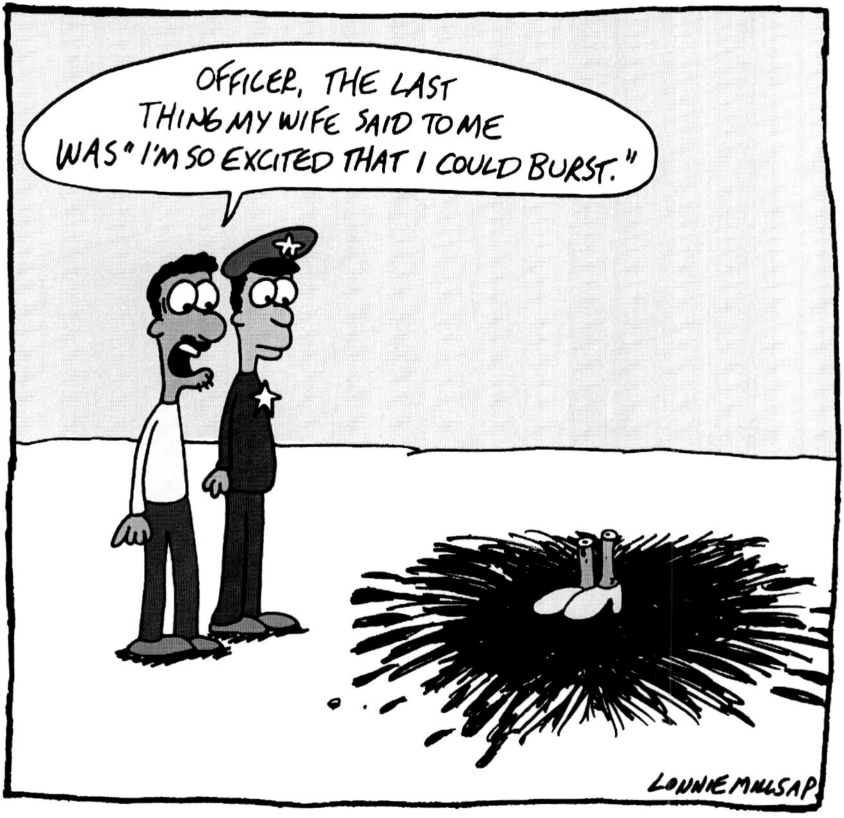
OFFICER, THE LAST THING MY WIFE SAID TO ME WAS "I'M SO EXCITED THAT I COULD BURST."
LONNIE MILLSAP

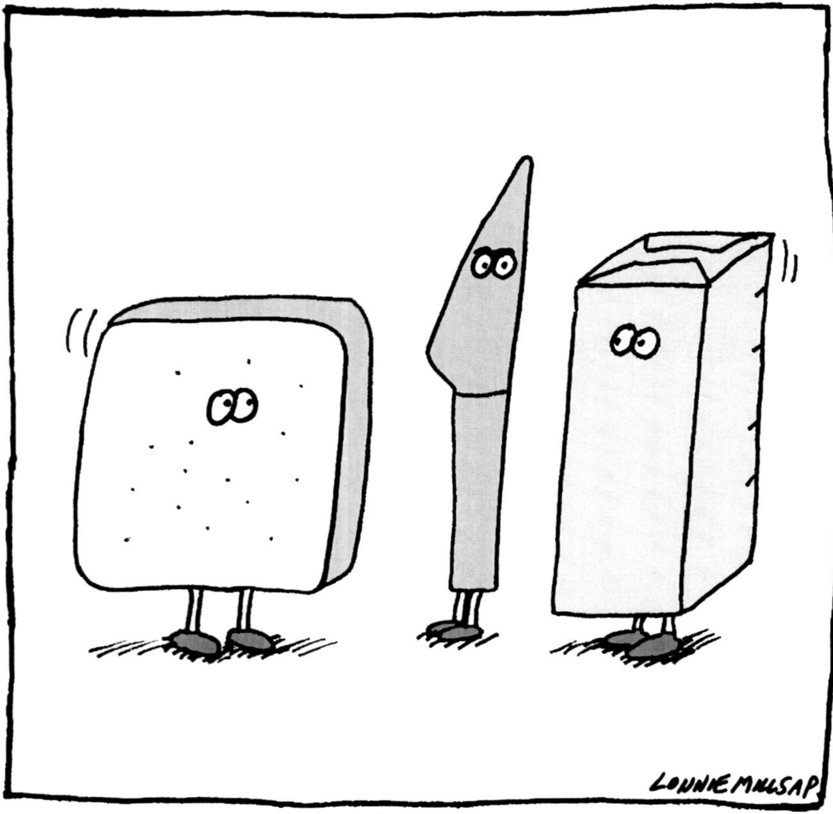
LONNIE MILLSAP

KNIFEY'S FRIENDSHIPS
NEVER LASTED VERY LONG

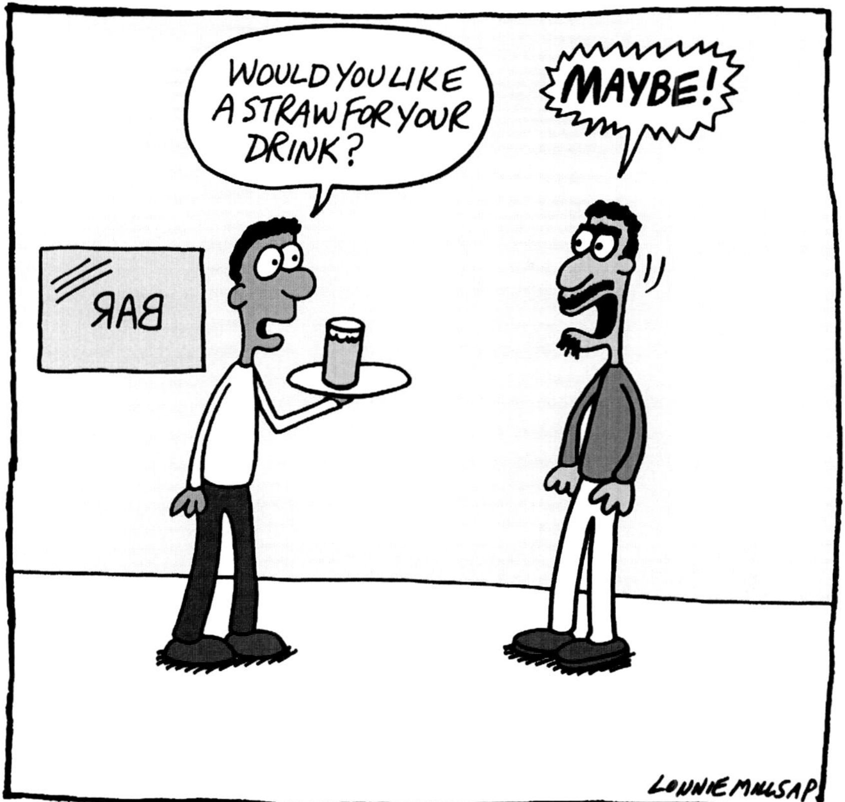
WOULD YOU LIKE A STRAW FOR YOUR DRINK?
MAYBE!
LONNIE MILLSAP

JAMAL JUST FINISHED TAKING HIS FIRST DAY OF ASSERTIVENESS TRAINING CLASS

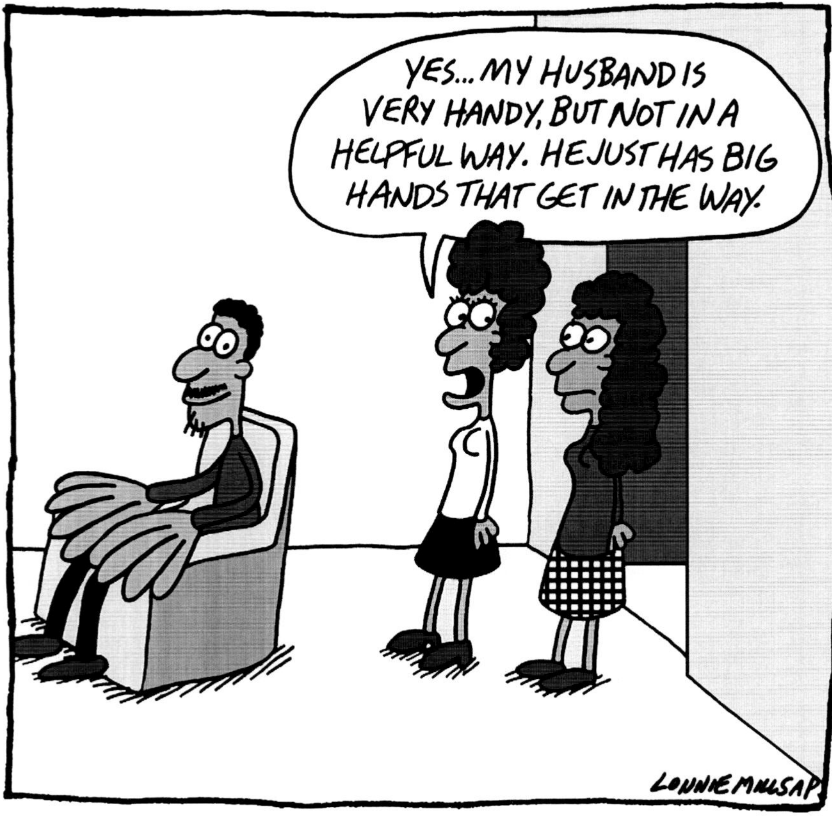
YES... MY HUSBAND IS VERY HANDY, BUT NOT IN A HELPFUL WAY. HE JUST HAS BIG HANDS THAT GET IN THE WAY.
LONNIE MILLSAP

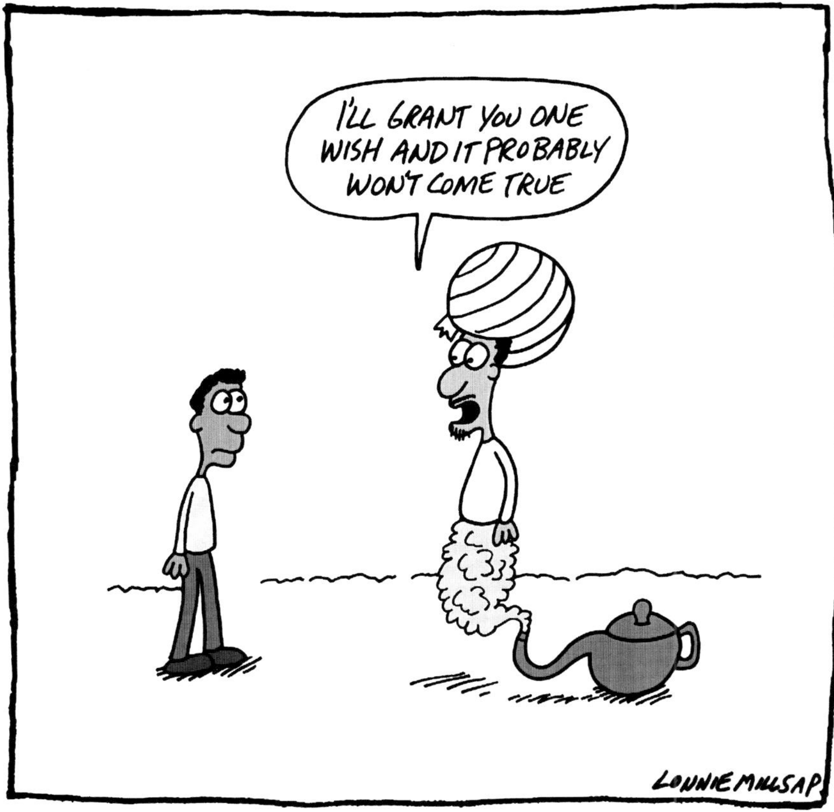
I'LL GRANT YOU ONE WISH AND IT PROBABLY WON'T COME TRUE
LONNIE MILLSAP

IF GENIES ORIGINATED IN DETROIT

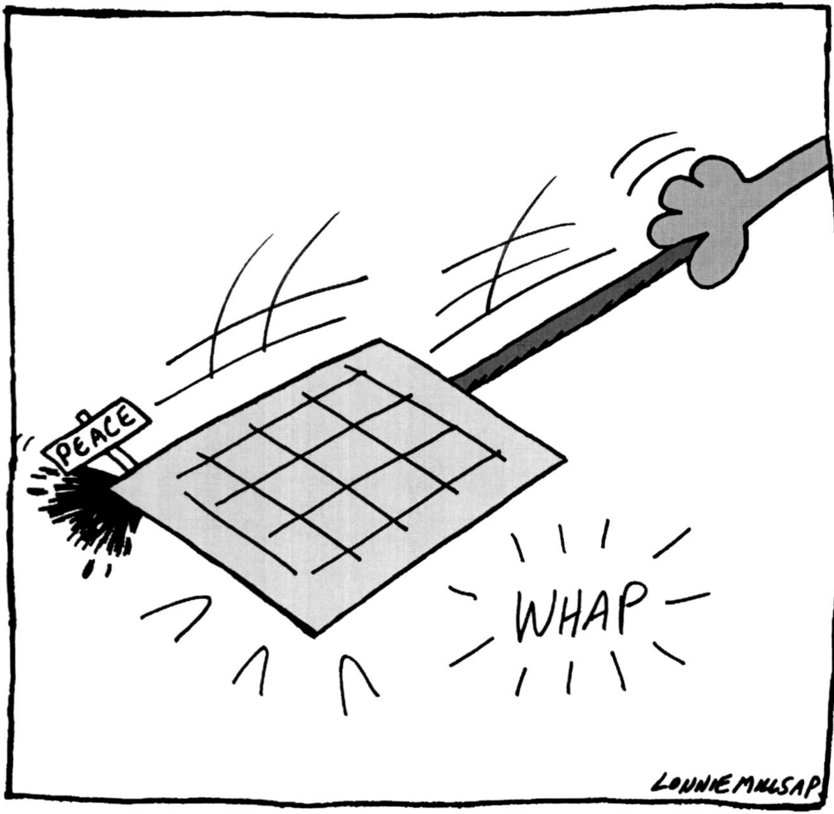
PEACE
WHAP
LONNIE MILLSAP

PROOF THAT FLY ACTIVISTS ARE NOT TAKEN SERIOUSLY

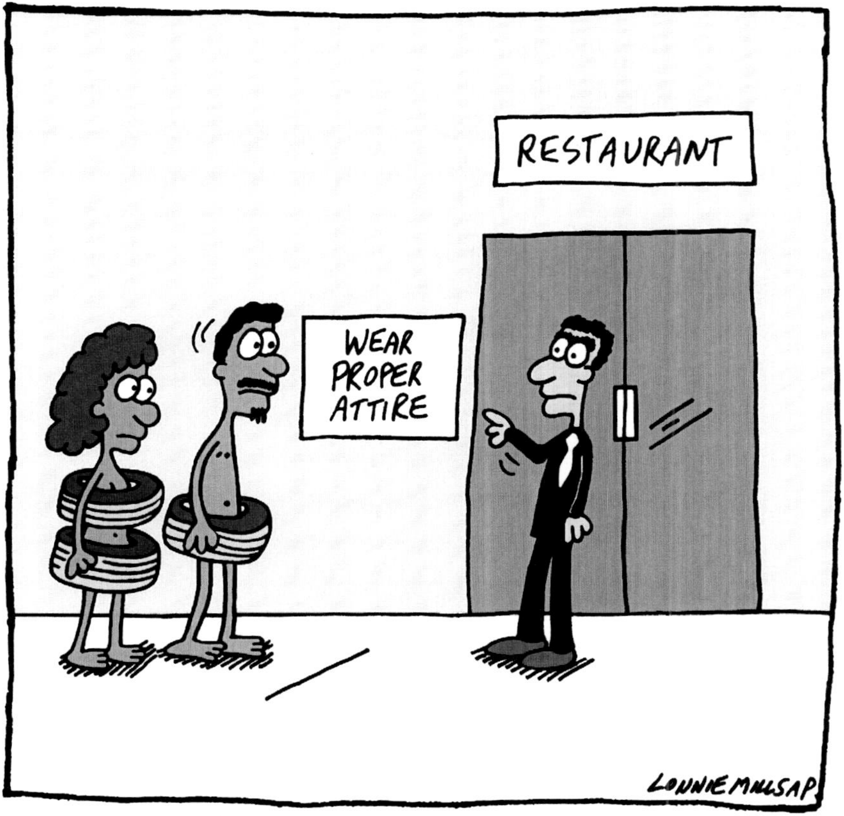
RESTAURANT
WEAR PROPER ATTIRE
LONNIE MILLSAP

BOB AND HIS WIFE THOUGHT THE SIGN SAID 'WEAR A PROPER TIRE.'

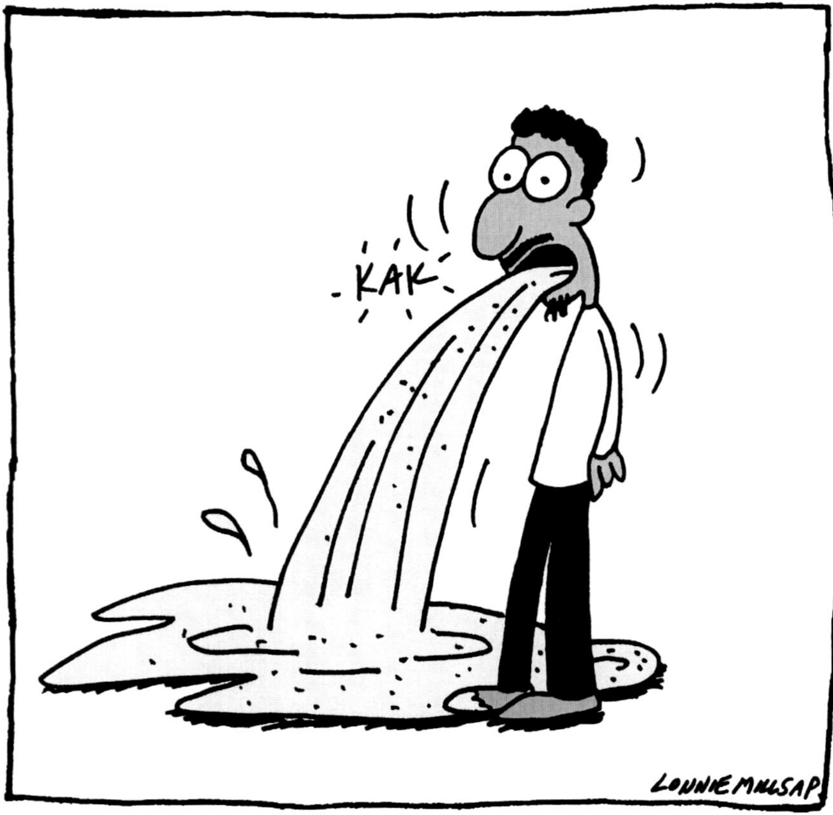
KAK
LONNIE MILLSAP

WHERE OATMEAL COMES FROM

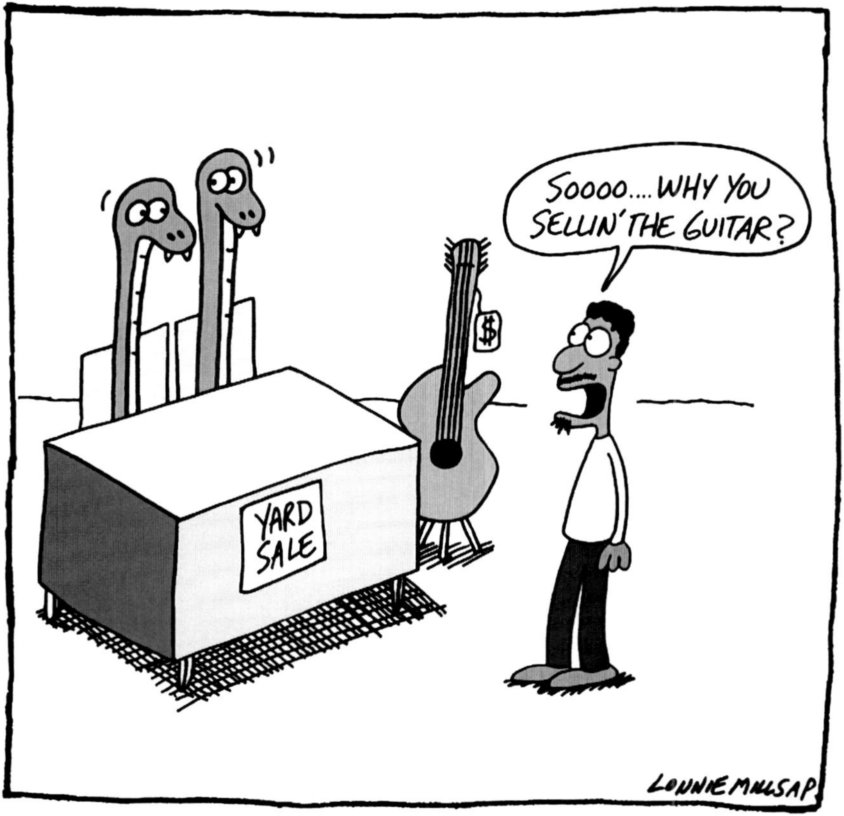
SOOOO.....WHY YOU SELLIN' THE GUITAR?
YARD SALE
$
LONNIE MILLSAP

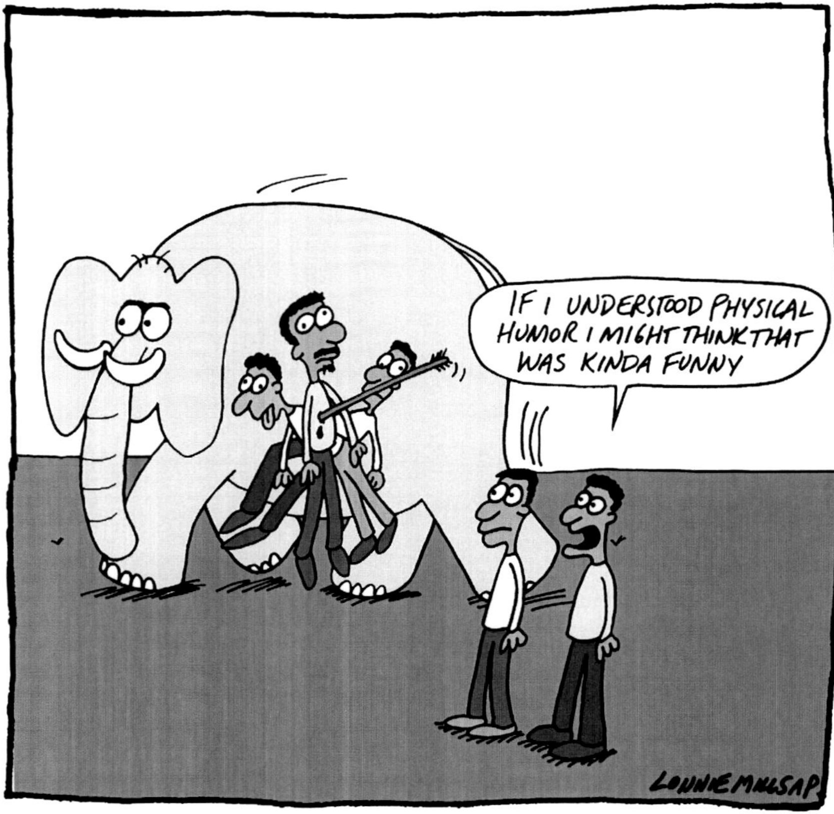
IF I UNDERSTOOD PHYSICAL HUMOR I MIGHT THINK THAT WAS KINDA FUNNY
LONNIE MILLSAP

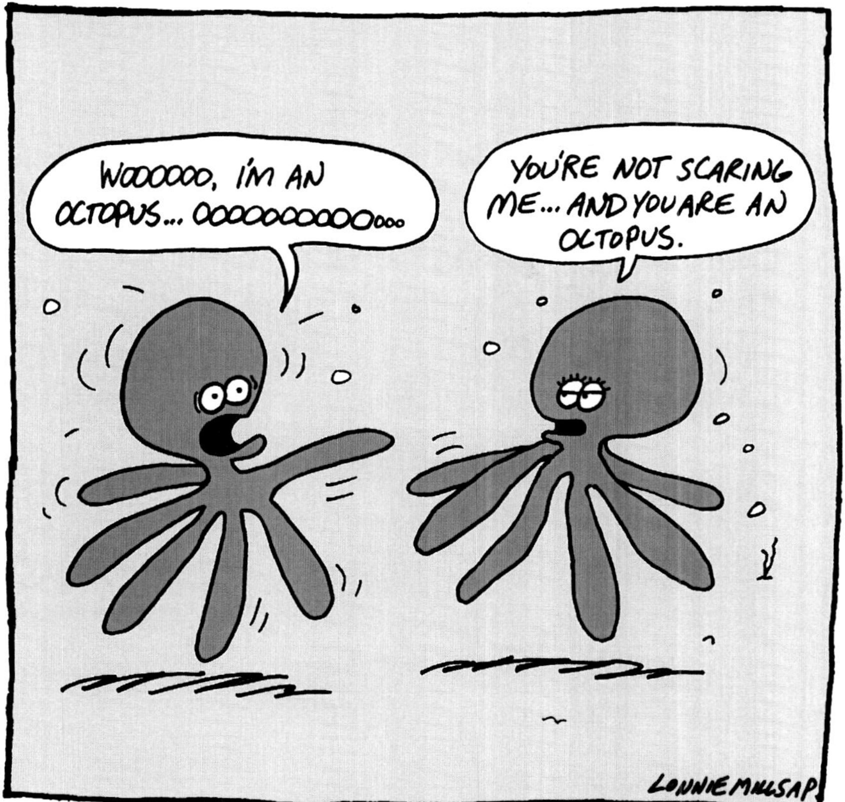
WOOOOOO, I'M AN OCTOPUS... OOOOOOOOOOOooo
YOU'RE NOT SCARING ME... AND YOU ARE AN OCTOPUS.
LONNIE MILLSAP

HALLOWEEN AT THE BOTTOM OF THE SEA

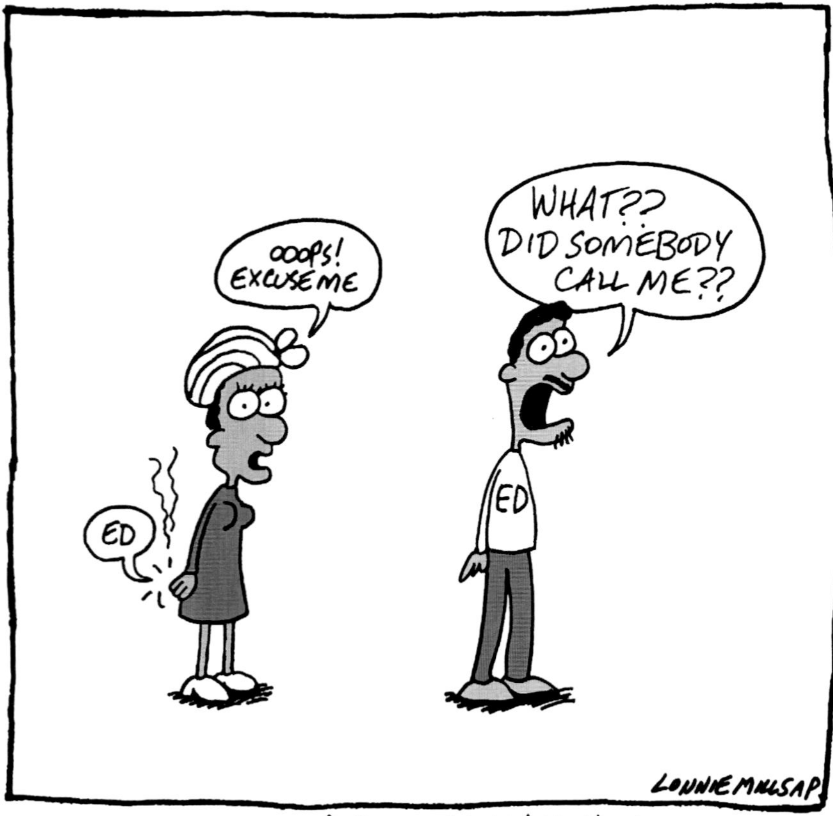
OOOPS! EXCUSE ME
ED
WHAT?? DID SOMEBODY CALL ME??
ED
LONNIE MILLSAP

CARTOON FLATULENCE WILL NOW BE REFERRED TO AS "ED"... MUCH TO ED'S DISMAY

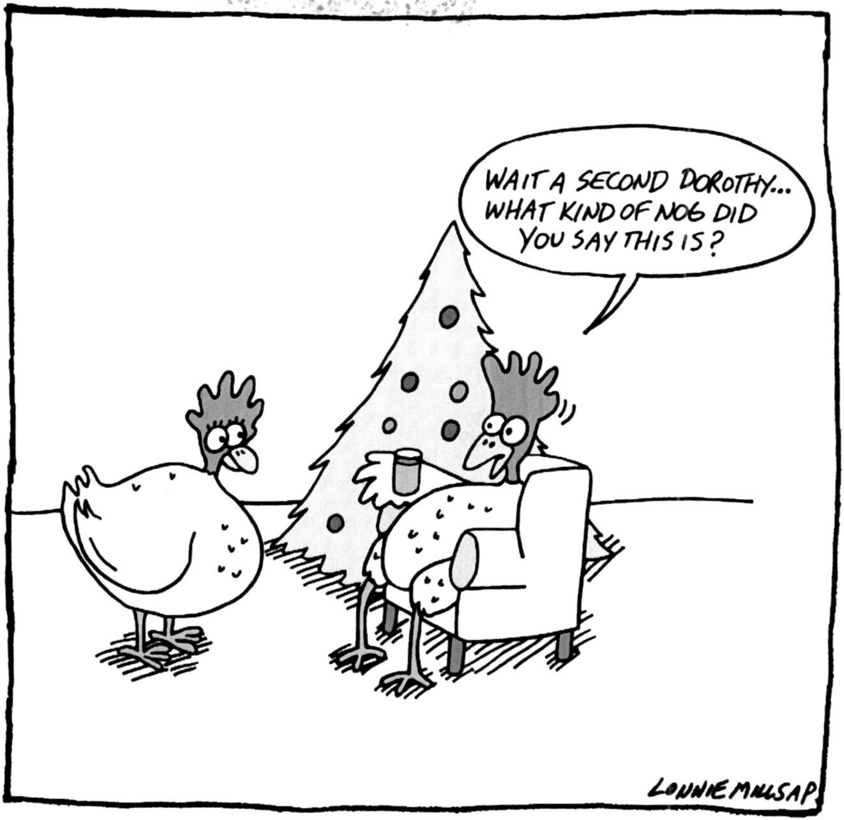
WAIT A SECOND DOROTHY...
WHAT KIND OF NOG DID
YOU SAY THIS IS?
LONNIE MILLSAP

THE BEGINNING AND END OF A HOLIDAY TRADITION

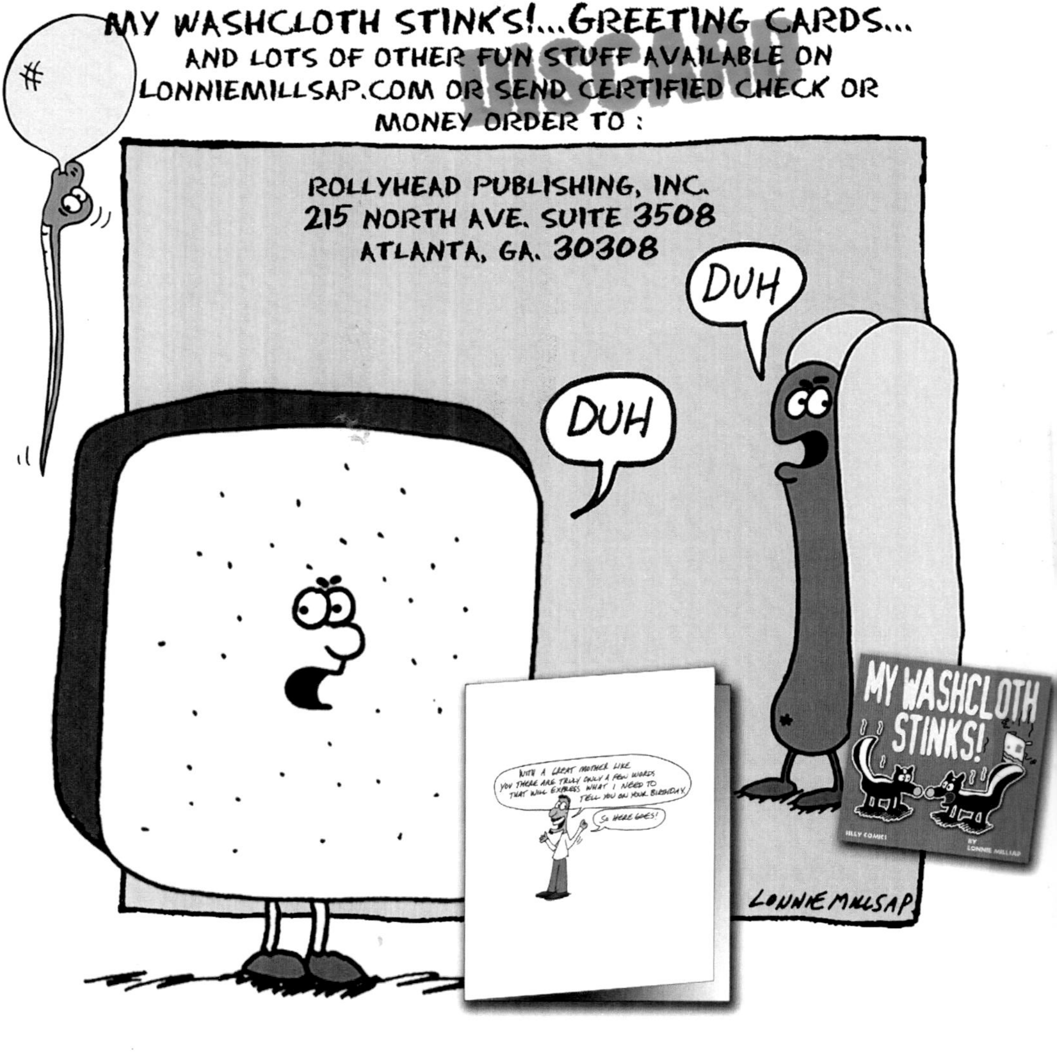
MY WASHCLOTH STINKS!...GREETING CARDS...
AND LOTS OF OTHER FUN STUFF AVAILABLE ON
LONNIEMILLSAP.COM OR SEND CERTIFIED CHECK OR
MONEY ORDER TO :
ROLLYHEAD PUBLISHING, INC.
215 NORTH AVE. SUITE 3508
ATLANTA, GA. 30308
DUH
DUH
WITH A GREAT MOTHER LIKE YOU THERE ARE TRULY ONLY A FEW WORDS THAT WILL EXPRESS WHAT I NEED TO TELL YOU ON YOUR BIRTHDAY.
SO HERE GOES!
MY WASHCLOTH STINKS!
SILLY COMICS
BY LONNIE MILLSAP
LONNIE MILLSAP